REFRESHED
PARABLES

REFRESHED PARABLES

CHARLES MILLS

Pacific Press®
Publishing Association

Nampa, Idaho | Oshawa, Ontario, Canada
www.pacificpress.com

Cover design by João Luiz Cardozo
Inside design by Aaron Troia

The author assumes full responsibility for the accuracy of all facts and quotations as cited in this book.

All Scripture quotations are taken from *The Easy English Clear Word*, a new simplified paraphrase of Scripture by Jack Blanco.

You can obtain additional copies of this book by calling toll-free 1-800-765-6955 or by visiting http://www.adventistbookcenter.com.

Library of Congress Cataloging-in-Publication Data

Names: Mills, Charles, 1950- author.
Title: Refreshed parables : Jesus' stories retold / Charles Mills.
Description: Nampa : Pacific Press Publishing Association, 2018.
Identifiers: LCCN 2017052623 | ISBN 9780816363490 (pbk. : alk. paper)
Subjects: LCSH: Jesus Christ—Parables—Juvenile literature.
Classification: LCC BT376 .M545 2018 | DDC 232.9/54—dc23 LC record available at
    https://lccn.loc.gov/2017052623

January 2018

Dedication

To Dorinda, the star of my personal parable

Contents

Introduction

Do you like stories? Of course. You're a kid! Well, I must be a kid, too, because I also *love* them!

It seems we're in good company. Jesus loved stories and told lots of them. Each one was designed to do something important in the heart of every man and woman, boy or girl who took the time to listen. They taught important lessons about why Jesus came to earth, what the kingdom of heaven was like, and how we should treat other people. The stories He shared reminded everyone how much God loves us all and how we should always love and respect others.

I became very excited when someone asked me, "What kind of stories do you think Jesus would tell today if He were here on earth? How would He teach His important lessons using modern illustrations and modern people?" Wow! What a great idea!

So I got busy and wrote the stories you're about to read. I hope you enjoy these *refreshed* parables that attempt to teach us the same lessons Christ's parables taught, but use today's culture and situations. Ask God to help you learn what you need to know to make your journey through life as fun and as satisfying as possible.

So what are we waiting for? Let the refreshed parables begin!

Wise Wes

MATTHEW 7:24–29

Well I think it looks really dumb," Zack declared, scratching his head and then replacing his baseball cap. "I mean, what's with those boards over there? They ruin the whole look, jutting out like that."

"Well, for *now*," Wes responded, mumbling his words past the row of nails protruding from between his lips. "They're what the plans called for."

"Plans?" his companion gasped. "You're using plans?"

"Of course. I don't know how to build a tree house. Do you?"

"Piece of cake," Zack stated with confidence. "You find a picture of one you like on the internet, then you build it. Duh!"

Wes took careful aim and hammered a long nail through one of the supports of his project, making sure the board remained parallel to the ground. His stepladder creaked and groaned with each strike. "I guess I'm not as creative as you," he admitted. "I gotta follow plans. That's them over there. See?" He aimed the handle of his hammer at a detailed set of drawings resting on the ground. "Tells you exactly where and how to build it. First, you put up these eight overlapping horizontal supports—that's a fancy name for these two-by-fours. Then you—"

"Spare me the details," Zack interrupted, lifting his hands. "I don't have time to give boards ridiculous names or read silly plans written by some guy who thinks he knows everything. We're building tree houses, not skyscrapers. I'll just do it my way and will probably be sipping a cool glass of lemonade on my front deck long before you even get to page two of your dumb plans. See ya later!"

With that, Zack hurried off toward his own yard, laughing not-so-quietly to himself.

Wes watched him go. Maybe his friend was right. Maybe he should build his tree house without using a set of plans. After all, what did the guy who made those drawings know about what he wanted? Was he going to let some stranger dictate how his tree house should look and how he should build it? What if those plans didn't match his dream of a place where he could escape from his younger sister? No one on earth knew better what he needed more than he.

He stopped hammering and stood balancing on his dad's stepladder for a long moment. *But then again*, he thought, *I really, really, really don't know how to build a tree house. A kite? No problem. Putting up shelves in my bedroom to hold my baseball trophies—both of them? I'm totally there! But building a tree house? Not so much.* The boy sighed. *I guess I'd better stick with those plans. And, if they tell me to "secure four overlapping sets of two horizontal supports," then that's exactly what I'd better do.*

Two weeks later, after a particularly bad summer storm had blown through the area, Wes stopped by Zack's home to check out his completed tree house. Both had finished their projects a few days earlier and were anxious to inspect each other's handiwork. He found his friend standing amid a pile of lumber in the backyard. "Hey Zack," he called out. "I thought you finished your house."

"I did," came the somewhat somber reply.

"Well, where is it?" Wes asked, surveying the broad, sturdy limbs above their heads.

"It's right here," his companion said, pointing at the twisted pile of boards at his feet. "It used to be up there." He motioned upward. "Now, it's down here."

"What happened?"

Zack shrugged. "The storm. All that wind and rain that came through last night?"

"Oh, that's a shame," Wes said. "I'm sorry, Zack."

"Yeah, well, like they say in Kansas, I will rebuild."

Wes shook his head sadly, then brightened. "So do you want to come over to my place this afternoon? We can hang out in my tree house."

"Your tree house?" Zack blinked. "You mean, like, up in the tree?"

"That's usually where people put them."

"Uh . . . yeah . . . sure!"

The two started walking down the driveway. After a long moment, Zack spoke. "By the way, Wes, do you still have those tree house plans?"

"Yup."

"Good," the boy said.

That day, two friends spent the entire afternoon up in Wes's tree house, enjoying the view and savoring the sweet taste of lemonade.

Matthew 7:24–29

"Those who obey Me are like the man who built his house on a rock. Heavy rains poured down. Flood waters rose. Strong winds blew and blew! But the house built on the rock stood firm.

"Those who say they love Me, but don't obey Me are like a man who built his house on sand. When the rains came and the winds blew, the house came crashing down."

When Jesus finished teaching, the people just sat there. They liked the simple way He said things, which was so different from the way the leaders and teachers said things. They could understand what Jesus said. It gave them hope and courage and wasn't just a lot of hard-to-understand rules.

Parable 1—Wise Wes

God wants me to build my life on the firm foundation of His love using the Bible as my "blueprint" for living.

1. I believe these are three of the most important foundation stones on which I should build my life. If I use them, my life will be happy and meaningful.

    * _____

    * _____

    * _____

2. Here are three "sandy" foundations on which the devil wants me to build my life. If I use them, my life will probably be sad and hopeless.

    * _____

    * _____

    * _____

3. Bible stories help teach me about God and how much He cares for me. My favorite is the one about _____. I know he or she used God's plans for building his or her life because _____.

4. Whenever I make a mistake and feel sad and afraid—like I'm on a shaky foundation—I immediately _____.

5. The best way for me to show others God's powerful plan for living is to _____.

Truth and Lies

MATTHEW 13:24–30

W hat else does it say?"

Jonathan shook his head slowly from side to side. "It says I'm a donkey."

"A donkey?"

"Yup. A donkey with big floppy ears."

Alex grinned. "Well, your ears *are* kinda big."

Jonathan laughed, then frowned. "Not you too!"

His friend lifted his hands defensively. "I'm sorry. I'm sorry. As your campaign manager, I shouldn't focus on your unique body parts. I should concentrate on the great things you're going to do for South-Central Middle School when you're elected student body president. Things like more fruit in the cafeteria, newer instruments for the band, and a replacement for that noisy window air conditioner in the science lab. The fact that someone writes crazy things about you on our campaign posters shouldn't concern me at all."

"The poster by the front entrance says my campaign manager is a sea slug."

Alex gasped. "OK, now he's gone too far!"

"How do you know the writer is a *he*?"

"Because all the girls like your ears. They think they're cute."

"They do?" Jonathan blinked. "How do you know?"

"I hear talk."

The candidate sighed. "So, if it's a he, which he is it? Who's trying to spread nasty rumors about me by writing lies on my campaign posters?"

"An enemy hath done this," Alex declared, trying to sound like a Shakespearian actor. "An enemy of the truth!"

"Hey guys." Larry McDonald strode into the classroom and tossed his backpack on a nearby chair. "How's the ol' campaign going?"

"It's going just fine," Alex said coldly. "I guess I should ask you the same question."

"My campaign?" the new arrival responded with a slight sneer on his face. "Oh, I've got this whole student body president thing in the bag. I'm as good as elected. Seems somebody's going around writing really nasty stuff about your man Jonathan and people are beginning to believe it. I just gotta sit back and enjoy the ride."

"They're just words," Alex asserted.

"Yeah, right," Larry chuckled, "Like the Declaration of Independence is *just words*."

* * * * *

That evening, Jonathan looked across the supper table at his father. "So, what should I do?" he asked. "It's not fun having rumors and lies written about you on your own campaign posters. And they're the only posters we have! We spent a lot of money on them. Poster board and art paint aren't exactly cheap, you know."

His dad thought for a long moment. "Don't do anything," he finally said. "Just let your campaign promises and those lies hang together until the election. If you took them down now, you'd be removing the truth about you as well as the lies. Besides," the man took a sip of water and studied his son thoughtfully, "truth has a way of surviving. I think the kids at your school will be more interested in what you *do* than what you say you're going to do."

A grin slowly creased the boy's face. "Wait a minute," he said. "I see where you're going with this. Thanks, Dad!"

Jonathan jumped up from the table and headed for his bedroom, punching in the phone number of his campaign manager as he ran down the hall.

* * * * *

The next day, the students at South-Central Middle School saw a strange sight as they entered the cafeteria for lunch. Jonathan stood by the serving counter offering each hungry scholar a shiny red apple. "Fruit is good for you," he told each person. "Elect me student body president and I'll work hard to get more fruit for your lunch tray every day."

That afternoon, the classmates heard a trumpet being played in the hallway between periods. "We need better instruments," Jonathan called out between trills, his lips ringed by the impression of a mouthpiece. "Elect me president, and I'll convince the band leader to let us hold a concert to raise funds. And, if elected, I'll stop playing the trumpet in the hallway." Everyone cheered.

Later, in science lab, students found Jonathan hard at work with the school custodian trying to repair the window air conditioner. He didn't say anything. Even if he had, no one would have heard him because the unit was too noisy. But everyone got the message.

* * * * *

A week later, the election results were posted on the bulletin board. Jonathan won by a landside!

Matthew 13:24–30

Then Jesus told them another story. "The kingdom of God is like a farmer who sowed good seed in his field. But during the night, his enemy came and sowed weeds all over the farmer's field. When the good seed came up, so did the weeds.

"Then the field workers went to the owner and said, 'You gave us good seed to sow, but the field is full of weeds. Where did they come from?' The owner answered, 'My enemy has done this.' The workers replied, 'Do you want us to go and pull up the weeds before they get too big?'

"The owner said, 'No. If you pull up the weeds, some of the wheat will come up with them. Let them grow together until the harvest. Then we will separate them. We'll store the wheat and burn the weeds.'"

Parable 2—Truth and Lies

The devil loves to tell lies about God. He started in heaven and continues here on earth. But I don't believe him.

1. The devil says God is unfair, but I know that He is always
   _____ because _____.

2. If someone says an unkind thing about me, the devil wants me to _____ but, instead, I
   _____.

3. Sometimes I'm tempted to spread a nasty rumor about a person at school. The person deserves to be embarrassed because of the way he or she has acted. But I've found the best thing to do, instead, is _____.

4. I believe that the main difference between a "weed" (something the devil sows) and "wheat" (what God sows) is
   _____.

5. Someday, all the "weeds" of the devil will vanish. This will happen when God _____.

Amber's Tiny Talent

MATTHEW 13:31, 32

Amber stood in the doorway of her school watching the parking lot. That was her assignment for the moment—to stand in the doorway and watch the parking lot. She sighed.

Everyone else in her art class was busy with their paintings—mounting their colorful creations in beautiful frames and hanging them proudly on the walls of the classroom in preparation for the arrival of a special visitor.

Amber had completed her painting right on time, but when the art teacher, Miss Anderson, asked her to identify her subject, she really wasn't sure. It was supposed to be a tree and a dog, but even she didn't know which was which. Her picture looked sort of like a dog with branches and a tree with a tail. The fact that she'd colored both red hadn't helped the situation in the slightest.

Earlier that year, both teacher and student had agreed that perhaps painting pictures wasn't high on her skills list and that she might be better off taking a music class. She'd auditioned for the school choir and discovered yet another talent she didn't have.

"Just call me 'no-talent Amber,'" the girl declared in frustration.

"Tell you what," Miss Anderson had asserted before art class began that day. "You can be the student representative to welcome world-renowned artist Percy Milton to our school when he comes to judge our art collection this afternoon."

That's why Amber was standing at the front door of the school, waiting for Mr. Milton's car to appear. She might not be able to draw or sing, but she could certainly say, "Welcome to Valley Middle School" and lead their guest to the classroom.

"Welcome to Valley Middle School," Amber enthused with a big smile as Mr. Milton exited his minivan. "My name is Amber, and I'll be happy to show you around."

"Well, thank you, Amber," Mr. Milton responded.

The girl noticed that her visitor was limping slightly. "Are you OK?" she asked.

"Oh this?" the man asked, pointing at his right knee. "It's just old age."

Amber frowned. "I'm so sorry. I'll be sure to walk nice and slow so you can keep up. We have a ramp by the front door so you won't have to climb any stairs. My grandfather has a bad knee too. Grandma says it's because he spent his whole life putting his foot in his mouth."

Mr. Milton chuckled as he walked, leaning heavily on a cane. "Tell me about your grandfather, Amber. He sounds like an interesting character."

"Oh he is! Almost as interesting as my uncle Sid!"

As the two made their way into the school, Amber entertained the visitor with vivid descriptions of her family, all the while making sure that Mr. Milton never fell behind or had to strain his hurting knee unnecessarily.

During the tour, they stopped to rest by the band room and listened to a tune being played. "I like that song," Amber said, tapping her foot almost in time to the melody. "It makes me think of ants marching up an anthill, each carrying a load of food for the hungry ant community. Do you like music, Mr. Milton?"

"Indeed I do," the man responded. "What else does it remind you of?"

And so it went; man and girl taking a tour of the school as Amber shared her thoughts, happily describing life along the building's cheery hallways.

Later at the art judging, Mr. Milton awarded prizes to three students, saying how lovely their paintings were. Then he surprised everyone with an announcement. "I'm adding another prize to our contest today," he told the class. "It goes to Amber."

"Amber?" the students gasped.

"Amber?" Miss Anderson blinked.

"Amber?" Amber breathed, eyes opening wide. "Mr. Milton, I don't have any art talent."

"Oh, but you do," Mr. Milton asserted. "Only, when you paint, you don't use pigments and brushes. You use words. This afternoon, your talent formed delightful images of this school for me. It created wondrous visions shaped by music and let me see the warm character of your family. Simple, kind, caring words—spoken in love—can fill the whole earth with beauty and joy. What may seem small, can become a great blessing to many, many people."

That night, Amber's mom asked her what she had done to deserve her prize. "Nothing special," the girl said with a smile. "I just talked."

Matthew 13:31, 32

Then Jesus told the people another story. "God's kingdom is like a tiny mustard seed, which a man planted in his garden. The tiny seed sprouted and grew, until the plant became the tallest one in the garden. The birds thought it was a little tree, so they built their nests there."

Parable 3—Amber's Tiny Talent

The size of a person or talent doesn't matter to God. Even though I'm young and still in school, God has many things waiting for me to do for Him.

1. My main talent is _____. I can use this talent—even though it may be small compared to another person's talent—to serve God by _____.

2. Sometimes I see a classmate trying to do something in class but not doing it very well. Instead of making fun of them, I _____.

3. I have a few talents that are growing fast. I've discovered that the two best ways to make any talent grow are to

   • _____

   • _____

4. My faith in God, like my talents, can grow stronger if I

   • _____

   • _____

5. It always amazes me that a tiny seed can become a giant plant. All it takes is

   • _____

   • _____

   • _____

Party Pooper

MATTHEW 18:12–14

Sam surveyed the room contentedly, so much fun, so much food, so many friends! His birthday party was going great. Mom had outdone herself with the little sandwiches, awesomely decorated cake, and heaping bowls of delicious dairy-free ice cream. Turning twelve had never been more exciting for anyone, he was sure.

He watched his friends interacting with each other. Todd was telling a funny story to Jared and Jasmine—something about a dog and a bird. Alisa was happily playing charades with a group of fellow classmates. Alex was, as usual, tucked away in the corner of the den reading a book. Yes, everyone was having a wonderful time. Everyone, that is, except—

"Hey, has anyone seen Thomas?" Sam called out. First one then another of his guests shrugged. "He was here earlier," Todd responded, putting his story on hold for a moment. Alisa shook her head. Alex looked around the room and then back down at his book. "I think I heard him say something about his Grandma," he muttered. "Oh and Todd told him he was no fun."

Todd chuckled. "Well all he was doing was sitting by the window sulking," he stated defensively. "This is supposed to be a party, not a funeral!"

Sam nodded as the noise in the room returned to party levels once more. But something wasn't right. *Why would Thomas be sulking?* he thought to himself. *He can be kinda shy, but I've never seen him—*

"Are you having a good time?" Mom asked as she hurried by carrying yet another tray of delicious treats to deliver to the guests.

"I'm having a *great* time," Sam assured her with a broad smile. "Thanks, Mom. You're the best!"

But, even as he spoke, the boy couldn't help but feel a little concerned. One of his friends—a rather strange, shy friend who lived nearby—was missing, and he didn't know why.

* * * * *

Thomas looked up from his computer screen when he heard a soft knock on his front door. "Who is it?" he called out.

"It's me, Sam."

The boy blinked. "Sam? Aren't you supposed to be having a birthday party?"

"May I come in?"

Thomas walked across the living room and opened the front door. "What are you doing here?"

"That's exactly what I wanted to ask you," his visitor responded.

The two neighbors stared at each other for a moment, then Thomas waved him in. "I . . . I had to take care of my grandma while my parents went to the store."

"OK. But their car is in the driveway. They're back."

Thomas sighed. "Look, Sam, I just didn't feel comfortable at your party. Know what I mean?"

"No."

"I'm not like your other friends," he continued. "They . . . they think I'm dumb or strange because I don't know how to tell funny stories, play silly games, or discuss the latest scientific breakthroughs like Alex. I'm just boring ol' me."

Thomas paused. "I didn't want to spoil your party, so I left."

Sam thought for a long moment and then sat down on the arm of the couch. "You're right," he said, nodding his head. "You're quiet, shy, kinda strange, and don't fit in too good at school. And—I gotta say—you're not exactly a fun person at parties either."

Thomas lowered his gaze. "I'm sorry," he said quietly.

A smile played at the corners of Sam's lips. "You're also honest, hardworking, and know more about taking care of old people than anyone I know. You never make fun of the kids at school, and when I tell you a secret, you don't blab it around like the others. I can trust you, I mean really *trust* you. And if you don't come back to my party right now, I'll go in there and tell your grandma!"

Thomas smiled in spite of himself. "You mean it?"

"*Yes!*" Sam declared. "All except the grandma part."

The boy grinned broadly. "Thanks, Sam," he enthused. "I did get you a gift, but it's not cool like everyone else's. It's a big belt buckle with a horse on it."

"Fine," Sam said. "And next year you can get me a big belt to go with it. Now let's go!"

A few minutes later, Sam contentedly surveyed the room filled with birthday guests. Everyone was there. Everyone.

Matthew 18:12–14

"If a man has 100 sheep and one of them gets lost, what will he do? He will ask someone to watch the others while he goes to look for the one lost sheep. And when he finds it, he is happier over this one sheep than over all the others, because it's no longer lost. That's how it is with God. His heart longs for everyone who is lost, whether they're adults or children."

Parable 4—Party Pooper

I believe there are two kinds of people on this earth: those who love Jesus and those who don't. Well I can fix that!

1. Sheep who are "lost" have wandered away from the shepherd. People who are "lost" have wandered away from

   _____.

2. Being lost in a wilderness or a big city would make me feel

   • _____

   • _____

3. I think that, many times, people who don't know God probably feel

   • _____

   • _____

   • _____

4. I'm so glad that God comes looking for me whenever I wander away from Him. My bad habits or selfishness can make me feel totally lost, but then I hear Him calling to me. I usually hear His loving call when I

   • _____

   • _____

5. The best way for me to help someone who is lost is to

   _____.

The Pond

MATTHEW 20:1–16

M r. Jackson stood watching four young people who were hard at work hauling brush and cutting down small scrub trees. High above, a hot, early-morning sun shone down mercilessly. "I didn't even know this pond existed," he explained. "It was hidden by all this growth when I purchased the land earlier this year. But then I heard frogs singing in the spring. Where you have frogs, you have water. Where you have water, there's probably a pond. I checked and, sure enough, there's a small, spring-fed body of water hidden in here."

"And you say we can swim in it all summer long?" Kyle asked, wiping sweat from his brow. "All we have to do is clear away the vegetation?"

"The pond will be yours to enjoy," the man stated. "But first, you have to get this all cleaned out and safe to swim in."

"No problem," Pete called out, a smile creasing his dirt-streaked face. "For a summer of free swimming, I'd clean out Lake Erie."

"Me too," Sarah joined in.

"Same here," Elle agreed. "The town's public swimming pool is always crowded and noisy. An afternoon in a cool, country pond with my friends sounds like a lot more fun."

"Good," Mr. Jackson said with an encouraging smile. "You clean, you swim."

With that, he hurried away, leaving his busy recruits to the task at hand.

* * * * *

A few hours later, as the sun continued its assault on the land, two more young people appeared, saws and shovels in hand. "Mr. Jackson said we could work on the pond project with you guys. He said he'd trade our work for a summer of free swimming."

Kyle frowned slightly. "Well, OK. You guys can work on that corner over there. Lots of bulrushes to clean out."

"Great," one of the new arrivals enthused. "Man, I can feel that cool water on my skin already. Let me at those bulrushes!"

Pete glanced at Kyle, shrugged, and returned to his work.

* * * * *

A few hours after that, three more young people arrived at the work site. "Is this the pond project?" they called. "Mr. Jackson said we could help clean it out and then swim in it all summer long."

"Where were you this morning?" Elle asked under her breath, forcing a smile. "We could have used you earlier."

"Well," one of the new-arrivals responded, "we didn't hear about this until we ran into Mr. Jackson at the grocery store."

"And we jumped at the chance," his friend added. "A summer of free swimming. Excellent!"

With that, the three began hauling away the brush that Sarah had been cutting. "Don't work too hard," they heard her say, a touch of sarcasm in her voice. "The sun's very hot. It's been hot *all day long*."

"OK," they responded, a bit confused by her attitude. "We'll be careful."

* * * * *

An hour before sunset, two more young people showed up. "Is this the pond project with the summer of free swimming?"

Kyle said nothing. He just tossed a shovel and pair of hedge clippers in their direction.

* * * * *

"Well, well, well," Mr. Jackson enthused as he arrived at the end of the day. "There's my beautiful pond, all ready for summer swimming. You guys did a terrific job! Come back and enjoy it any time you want. You earned it."

Kyle, Pete, Elle, and Sarah stayed behind after the others left. They didn't look pleased. "What's the problem?" Mr. Jackson asked. "Did I work you too hard?"

"Mr. Jackson," Kyle asserted, "we worked here all day in the hot sun to get our summer of free swimming. But the guys who came later didn't work anywhere near as long as we did, yet they get to swim just like us. That's not fair."

The man thought for a moment. "Kyle," he said softly, "I made a promise to you, and I'm keeping it. I made promises to them, and I'm keeping those too. However, I think you'll discover that working long and hard for something makes that something much more valuable—no matter what it is. While everyone who was here today will enjoy the pond this summer, you four will enjoy it the most. Why? Because you put in more work, more straining, more sweating. This water will feel extra cool to your skin and bring you a much greater sense of satisfaction."

And it did.

Matthew 20:1–16

Jesus said, "God's kingdom is like the man who needed people to work in his vineyard. At six o'clock in the morning he found some men who wanted a job. He told them how much he would pay them for one day's work, and they agreed. Then he sent them into his vineyard to work.

"By nine o'clock he realized he needed more workers. So he went and found some more men looking for work. He offered to pay them a fair wage, and they agreed. Then he sent them to work in his vineyard.

"Soon he realized that he needed still more workers. At twelve o'clock and again at three o'clock he went to the marketplace for more workers. He offered to pay them what was fair, and they all agreed. Then he sent them into his vineyard to work.

"As late as five o'clock he went to get still more workers. When he found some, he asked, 'Haven't you found any work today?' They answered, 'No one has hired us.' The farmer said, 'You're hired. Come with me and help finish the harvesting. I'll pay you what's fair.' They agreed.

"When the work was done, the farmer told his supervisors to call the men together and pay them, starting with the last workers first. Each man was paid what the first men were promised.

"The first ones got excited, because they thought that if the farmer paid the last ones that much, they would get even more. But he paid them all the same. Then the first ones got upset.

"They told the farmer that he was unfair and said, 'These men came last and worked only a few hours, and you paid them as if they had worked all day. But we worked through the heat of the day, and you paid us only the same as you paid them!'

"The farmer asked, 'Why do you say that I was unfair? Didn't I pay you what we had agreed to? Be glad someone hired you. Take your pay and be happy. I decided to pay everyone the same. Don't I have a right to do what I want with my own money? Don't be jealous because I'm generous. Be glad that these workers could help finish the harvest!' "

Then Jesus said, "That's how it will be at the end. The first will be last, and the last first. Some work for what they can get, while others work because they love Me."

Parable 5—The Pond

The Bible tells me that God loves all people all of the time. He wants to reward us whenever we do something kind and loving and compassionate—no matter how long we've been doing it.

1. God is pleased when I do something good. When I forgive someone or help someone with a problem, I have two feelings in my heart that I know are from God:

   • _____

   • _____

2. Many jobs God gives me to do (like helping someone or sharing my blessings with others) are hard work. But I don't mind. Working hard for God brings rewards both now and _____.

3. I know that working for God won't earn me one single day in heaven. Jesus' sacrifice on the cross is what made all of that possible. But I can begin to enjoy God-given rewards right here on earth. These rewards include

   • _____

   • _____

4. When I see a person who serves God begin to grow tired or sad, I help him or her by _____.

5. The reward I'm looking forward to the most in heaven is _____.

PARABLE 6

The Quiz

MATTHEW 25:1–13

W hat's the capital of Peru?"

Jason looked up from his social studies book. "What'd you ask?"

"What's the capital of Peru?" Lisa repeated. "I'm thinking Bolivia."

"Bolivia's a country, not a city," Mark asserted, shaking his head in disbelief. "The capital of Peru is Lima."

"*Argh!*" Lisa growled. "Why do we need to study Peru anyway? It's not like any of us are ever going down there."

"We're studying Peru because Mrs. Tollerton said to study Peru," Jason stated matter-of-factly. "She's the teacher. We're the students. End of story."

Mark glanced out the window and sighed. "Just look at them," he breathed, "our classmates running around, having fun, playing ball, *not* studying social studies. And here we are, holed up in this library like fugitives hiding from justice."

"Well," Jason said, "I guess they're not worried about the quiz like we are. They probably already know what the capital of Peru is."

"Lima," Lisa muttered under her breath. "It's Lima—like that's important to anyone except people who live in Peru. *They* need to know that—not us!" She lifted her hand. "OK, now everybody hush up. I've got to learn more about this wonderful country that I'll never see in my entire life."

The three friends bent over their textbooks and tried to stuff their brains with last-minute facts and figures relating to that far-away country.

The pictures highlighted in the textbook and on the library computer screens seemed like they could have been taken on another planet. Everything about Peru was different from their home state of Kansas. Towering mountains; deep, green valleys; desert terrains; colorful clothes, strange animals—even the food looked weird. But like Jason said, if Mrs. Tollerton told everyone to study Peru, that's exactly what they were going to do. The three friends certainly didn't want to flunk social studies. That would be a lot worse than missing a few ballgames. Besides, if they flunked, they'd have to study about Peru all over again next year.

* * * * *

When Mrs. Tollerton's students filed into the classroom after recess, they were greeted by a covered whiteboard with some writing peeking out around the edges. "The quiz!" everyone groaned.

"I forgot!" some shrieked.

"I'm dead," others moaned.

"Hey Jason," Carl cried out, "tell me everything you know about Peru *right now!*"

"Hey, go to the library like we did," Jason responded. "You've got four minutes before class. Use the computer. Look it up!"

A group of classmates who'd heard their conversation hurried out behind Carl, eager to do a quick review of the subject.

When the class bell rang, they hadn't returned. Mrs. Tollerton strode into the room and smiled at those who remained. "As promised," she announced cheerily, "here's your quiz on Peru. I've tried to highlight the most important points as outlined in your textbook. Good luck!"

With that she removed the covering from the whiteboard. Everyone read the first question and then bent over their test papers, pencils poised, planning their first answer.

A few minutes later, voices sounded in the hallway, beyond the closed door. "We've got to get inside," they heard Carl plead. "We've got to take that quiz!"

But the ever-present hall monitor refused to let them enter. "The test has already begun," she stated firmly. "No admittance! Those are the rules."

For the rest of the period, Jason, Lisa, and Mark searched their memories to form answers to the questions on the whiteboard. Some came easily. Others took a little more concentration. But everything the teacher was asking sounded familiar. They'd read about it. They'd seen pictures of it. Or they'd heard stories about it in class. All they had to do was match those printed words, colorful images, and spoken facts with the various questions on the quiz.

When it was all over, the three friends sighed deep, satisfying sighs. They may not have earned a scholarship to Yale that day, but they knew they'd managed to answer most questions correctly.

Looking up from their papers, they saw Mrs. Tollerton standing with a new student to introduce to the class. "This is Alfredo," the teacher announced. "He just moved here from Peru, the country we're studying. Anyone have any questions for him?"

Lisa quickly fluffed her hair and adjusted her blouse. This new guy was *cute*! "I have a question," she called out. Staring straight at the stranger and smiling sweetly, she asked, "Have you ever been to Lima?"

Matthew 25:1–13

Then Jesus told His disciples three stories. He said, "During the time of the end, My people will be like ten bridesmaids who took their lamps to wait for the bridegroom to come and pick up his bride. Five of these bridesmaids were wise, and five were foolish. The foolish didn't take extra oil with them, but the wise did.

"The bridegroom was delayed. So while the bridesmaids waited, they all fell asleep. About midnight the bridegroom's coming was announced, and everyone wanted to go out to meet him. All the bridesmaids jumped up, lit their lamps, and went to welcome the bridegroom.

"But the lamps of the foolish bridesmaids started going out. So they said to the others, 'Please give us your extra oil, because our lamps are almost out.' The wise bridesmaids said, 'We would love to help you, but if we give you our extra oil there won't be enough for us. Hurry, go buy some oil for yourselves before it's too late.'

"While the foolish bridesmaids were away buying oil, the bridegroom came. The wise were so happy to see him. Then they all went inside, and the doors were closed.

"Soon the foolish came back and tried to get in, but the doors were locked. They knocked and said, 'Please open the doors and let us in!' The bridegroom said, 'I don't know you. All those who welcomed me are here, and my father has locked the doors.'

"That's how it will be at the end of the world. No one knows exactly when I will come back."

Parable 6—The Quiz

Sometimes people ask me, "Are you ready for Jesus to come?" Good question! Makes me think about what I need to be doing to prepare for His return.

1. The devil wants me to become lazy and not think about Christ's return, so he

   * _____
   * _____
   * _____

2. I've found the best way to stay ready for Jesus to come is to

   * _____
   * _____
   * _____

3. The oil in Christ's parable represents "faith." When we don't have faith, we can't keep our lives shining bright so that others can see the way to heaven. I've found that the very best way to keep my faith alive and shining brightly is to _____.

4. When I run out of faith, I immediately _____.

5. Three ways that I can help someone who is running low on faith are to

   * _____
   * _____
   * _____

PARABLE 7

Listening

MATTHEW 13:1–9

Jason watched the crumbling apartment buildings pass by the car window as his dad maneuvered their van along the trash-strewn street. He saw people dressed in soiled T-shirts and torn jeans and seated on cement steps or walking across grassless lawns. Rap music blared from somewhere nearby, and angry voices tossed obscenities into the humid air.

Jason didn't like coming here, but he knew that his dad had a passion for this neighborhood. "I grew up in that apartment building over there," his father announced, even though he knew he'd shared that bit of information with his son dozens of times before. "It was just Mom and us six kids. We were quite a bunch."

Jason frowned. "I wouldn't want to live here," he said, more to himself than to his dad.

"Neither do they," his father responded, motioning toward the people walking along the rutted sidewalks.

"So why don't they move away?" the boy asked. "You did."

"I was lucky," his father said. "My mom—your grandma—pushed me to get good grades and I was able to attend college and then medical school. Thankfully, I listened to her and worked hard. My brothers and sisters didn't."

"So is that why you come here each week—to show them that you're a doctor?"

"No. I come here because so many of these people are sick and need my help. Our church's free clinic depends on me to bring a little bit of healing and a little bit of God's love to this neighborhood. Besides, it makes me feel like I'm doing something worthwhile."

Jason was silent for a moment, then he pointed. "Hey, isn't that Mr. Miller over there—you know, the man you talked to last week at the clinic?"

"Poor guy is an alcoholic," Dad responded. "I shared with him some things he can do to stop drinking."

The boy frowned. "Well, it didn't work. Look at him staggering along."

His dad sighed. "I think you're right. Oh, too bad. Guess I need to talk to him some more!"

"And," the boy called out, "there's ol' Freddie in the alley. He's been coming to the clinic for months and you've been telling him how to lose weight so he can be healthy. But look at him. He's as big as ever with a cheeseburger in one hand and large soft drink in the other. Didn't you counsel him to eat fruit and drink water instead?"

"Sure did," his father said with a frustrated moan. "Told him to exercise more too. I don't think he listened to a word I said."

"And look at Mrs. Thomas over there by the lamp post. Isn't she going to have a baby, like—tomorrow?"

His father chuckled. "Well sometime within the next few weeks."

"Then why is she smoking a cigarette? I overheard you tell her three weeks ago that smoking is very harmful to her baby—and to her too. You even invited her to attend the stop smoking classes that Mrs. Greenfield holds at church, and she promised she'd attend. But she must not have. She's still smoking!"

Jason's father nodded. "That's really sad. I thought I'd gotten through to her." He paused. "Her poor baby will be born with some very dangerous health issues."

The boy looked over at his father. "So why are you here, Dad? Why do we leave our nice house on a nice clean street with nice, healthy people walking around and come down to your old neighborhood and try to get these guys to do something that will make them healthier? They don't listen! They just eat the free veggie sandwiches we serve and drink the fruit juice we offer, and then they go out and do what they've always done. To me the free clinic is a big waste of time."

His father thought for a moment. "But, Jason, some people do listen. Some people, such as Mr. Andrews and Mrs. Tam, do what I suggest. They've changed their diets and gotten their diabetes under control. And remember Terrance Potter? His heart was failing! But he learned to exercise more and eat right, and now he's doing great. And a few moms-to-be have learned to be healthier too. That's what makes it all worthwhile. As long as there are people who will listen, I'll show up each and every week to talk to them."

Jason nodded slowly. Then smiled. "OK, Dad," he said. "I hear ya."

Matthew 13:1–9

Then Jesus went outside to see His mother and step-brothers. They were worried that if He kept disagreeing with the leaders and priests, He would be arrested and killed. Jesus tried to explain, but they didn't understand. So He went down to the lake to get some peace and quiet.

But soon so many people came to see Him that they almost pushed Him into the water. So He got into one of the fishing boats and began telling them stories.

"Look. Up there on the hill a farmer is planting seeds. Once a farmer was sowing seeds like that.

"Some of the seeds fell on a path. The birds came and ate them. Some seeds fell on stony ground. They sprang up quickly, but the dirt wasn't very deep. The hot sun made the plants shrivel and die because their roots could not go down very far. Some seeds fell among weeds and thorns. They grew fast and soon choked the good seeds.

"But most of the seed fell on good soil, and the farmer usually had a good harvest. It brought him thirty, sixty, or even 100 times more than he had planted. Think about what I've said and learn a lesson about spiritual things."

Parable 7—Listening

Have you ever tried to tell something important to someone and they just ignored you? I have. Imagine how God feels when He wants to save our souls, and we demonstrate to Him that we have other "more important" things on our minds.

1. Which of these three are most important: making money, becoming famous, or heaven?

   _____

2. When I really want to hear what someone is saying, I

   - _____

   - _____

   - _____

3. Sometimes, God needs to tell me things I don't want to hear, such as when I've done something bad and He's trying to help me learn from my mistakes. Which of these means He loves me: When He's telling me how good I am or when He's telling me how sinful I am?

   _____

4. The devil doesn't want me to listen to God, so he

   - _____

   - _____

   - _____

5. People said mean things to Jesus. Did He ignore them, or did He listen and love them anyway? How did He show His love after He listened?

   _____

The Friendly Net

MATTHEW 13:47–50

P astor Toliver, we need to talk."

The minister looked down the length of his ladder to find Sarah Kim staring up at him. "Well, hello young lady," he mumbled, moving the words past the row of nails held tightly between his lips. "Mind if I finish installing this downspout first?"

"What?"

The man lifted a gloved hand to his mouth and removed the nails. "I said, mind if I finish repairing this downspout first? If I don't get this done, the next time we have a heavy rain during services, the entire congregation will get baptized whether they want to or not."

Sarah chuckled. Leave it to Pastor Toliver to find humor in a broken downspout. "Well, OK," she called back up the ladder. "I'll wait."

As promised, the pastor completed his work and then climbed down to ground level, a smile of satisfaction creasing his face. "Of course, I wouldn't mind baptizing the entire congregation," he said, dropping his tools into the toolbox. "Heaven knows some of us sure could use a refresher." He plopped down on the lawn beside the church and his young visitor joined him. "So what's up Sarah? You look worried."

The girl thought for a moment. "Remember what you said last month about being friendly to everyone?"

"Yes. Just as Jesus was friendly to everyone."

"Well, it doesn't work."

"It doesn't?"

"No. I decided to be friendly to everyone at school. I was even nice to Jennifer Haines, and she hates me."

"So what didn't work?"

"Now everyone wants to be my friend!"

The pastor frowned. "And that's a bad thing because—?"

"Because some of those 'friends' want me to do dumb stuff such as cut class with them or share my test answers or talk trash about people." The girl shook her head. "I'm not that kind of person, Pastor Toliver."

"I'm sure you're not."

"So what should I do? You told us to be friends with everyone but—"

"Wait a minute, Sarah," the man interrupted. "I didn't say be friends with everyone. I said *be friendly* with everyone. There's a difference."

"What do you mean?"

"Well, Jesus was certainly friendly with all the people He met. He visited the home of a dishonest tax collector, had heartfelt conversations with known sinners, prepared meals for anyone who was hungry, even treated the devil himself with a degree of courtesy. But He was very careful whom He allowed to be His close friends. He ended up with just twelve, and a couple of them even caused Him great sorrow. Peter denied knowing Him, and Judas arranged to have Him arrested and crucified. Each and every one of those disciples knew what Jesus was like. They understood that He had limits and they respected Him for it."

Sarah thought for a moment. "So what am I supposed to do with people who want to be my friend because I act friendly?"

"Well, go for it," Pastor Toliver said with a broad smile, "as long as they respect you and don't ask you to do things you don't want to do. Being friendly casts a pretty big net. It can scoop up all kinds of people. But don't forget who you are and what you believe. If your fellow classmates are drawn to you, make sure they understand who you are and what you will or won't do. Then if they still want to be your friend and are willing to respect your wishes, you've got yourself a true pal who will support you and not drag you down to his or her level."

The girl sat in silence for a long moment, then nodded slowly. "I think I understand." She frowned. "So is Jesus my friend?"

"Do you believe what He says in the Bible?"

"Yes."

"Do you love Him enough to let Him be who He is and respect and obey His commandments and principles instead of insisting on having your own way when you're around Him?"

"Yes."

"Then God's got Himself a true friend in you. You see, God will always be friendly to you—He's friendly to everyone. But if you're willing to go that extra mile, then you and He can be *forever* friends—and that's the best kind. He, like you, has cast His own net. But I think you want to be the kind of friend He can keep forever."

Sarah rose to her feet. "Thank you, Pastor Toliver."

"Happy fishing," the man said with a smile.

Matthew 13:47–50

"The kingdom of God is also like fishing with a net. When fishermen draw in their net, they find both good and bad fish in it. So they sort them out. They save the good fish and toss the bad ones back.

"That's how it will be at the end of the world. The

angels will do the sorting. They will take those who love
God and leave the others. The wicked will be burned up
and their lives will end forever."

Parable 8—The Friendly Net

Jesus says we should love all people—and that includes people who aren't nice to us or who don't love Jesus. Sometimes, that's not easy.

1. The Bible says that man (people) look at other people and judge them by what they see on the outside (the way they look and act). But God looks somewhere else before He makes a decision about that person. Where does God look (1 Samuel 16:7) and what does that mean?

   _____

   _____

2. According to this parable, what are we supposed to do with those who are unkind to us? Leave them alone or include them in our friendly net?

   _____

   _____

3. During the harvest (the second coming of Jesus), those who don't love God and who are unkind to us will be separated from us forever. But until then, what can we all do to show them God's love so that maybe they'll change their minds and learn to love Jesus?

   _____

   _____

4. I want to live and love like Jesus. How did He show people that He loved them?

   _____

   _____

5. Sometimes I feel like I'm not being a very good person. Does God still love me?

_____

_____

6. What should be my response to such a loving God?

_____

_____

The Facts

MATTHEW 13:44

Mark studied his reflection in the mirror and didn't like what he saw. His cheeks were puffy. His neck was puffy. As a matter of fact, his whole body was puffy.

"I'm puffy!" he said aloud as his mother entered the room.

The woman stopped and studied her son for a moment. "Well you have gained a little weight," she admitted.

"A *little* weight?" Mark responded. "Mom. I've gained a *lot* of weight. I'm almost two of me. My clothes don't fit anymore. What happened?"

His mother sighed. "It's my fault. Ever since I got the new job, I haven't taken the time to fix healthy meals. Instead, I bring home something from the fast food restaurant." She checked her reflection in the mirror. "I think I'm gaining weight too."

"The nurse at school said that being fat isn't healthy," Mark warned. "She said you can get sick and stuff. I don't want to get sick."

"Me either," the woman stated thoughtfully. "Without good health you can't do anything." Then she lifted her chin slightly. "OK, OK," she announced. "Let's look at the facts."

Mark smiled. His mom was a lawyer and was always "looking at the facts" whenever there was a problem needing to be solved. The "facts" had led them to this new town after Dad had died. The "facts" had sent his mom back to school to earn a law degree. The "facts" had helped them decide which school he was to attend, what type of house to rent, and even how much money to spend on clothes. He knew that "facts" were the most important part of decision-making, and he trusted his mom to use just the right ones for their situation.

"Fact number one," she began. "We weren't fat when I had a different job, and we ate mostly fruits and vegetables, right?"

"Right."

"Fact number two. Refined foods and dairy products contain a lot of saturated fat, sugar, and salt, which can make you gain weight, right?"

"Right."

"So what does that tell you?" the woman asked, pointing at her son the way she pointed at witnesses in the courtroom. "What do the facts reveal?"

Mark thought for a moment. "The facts say that we should move to Hawaii, live in a hut, and eat coconuts."

The woman laughed. "Or they indicate that I've been neglecting the most important part of our lives. I've got to make some serious changes to our lifestyle. Bottom line? We need to eat different food, exercise more, and lay off the junk."

Mark chuckled. "I like my Hawaii idea better."

"No, no, we can do this," Mom said, waving her hand in the air. "But it's going to take some work." She began to pace. "We know what we need to do. Now we just need to make sure nothing stands in our way. Health is the most valuable gift we have. We need to protect it at all costs. Do you or do you not agree?"

"Mom, we're not in court," Mark said, "and yes, I agree."

His mother lifted her index finger and wiggled it. "Then follow me," she ordered.

The two marched into the kitchen and the woman opened the refrigerator. "See all those frozen dinners packed with fat, sugar, and salt?"

"Yes."

"Toss 'em."

"Toss 'em?"

"Yep. In the trash."

Then the two hurried to the cabinets. "See all that packaged, chemical-filled, refined food up there?" the woman asked.

"Yes."

"Toss it."

"Just like the frozen dinners?"

"Exactly."

After the kitchen and pantry had been cleared of everything un-healthy, Mom wiggled her finger again. "Follow me," she said.

Mother and son drove to the grocery store and soon returned home with bags brimming with beans, fresh vegetables, ripe fruit, and small cans of nuts. Soon where there had been cow's milk, there was now almond milk. Where there had been frozen dinners, there were now containers of legumes and whole-grain rice. Where there had been refined foods, there were now whole plant foods. To Mark, it looked like they'd been attacked by a farmer.

"When you need to improve something valuable, such as health," his mother said later that evening as she stood at the stove stirring a delicious-smelling vegetable stew, "you can't go halfway. You've got to make a complete change—a *lifestyle* change. You have to get rid of what's wrong and replace it with what's right, understand?"

Mark nodded.

Mom sighed and grinned. "I rest my case."

Matthew 13:44

Jesus said, "The kingdom of God is like buried treasure. One day a man found it and quickly covered it up. He sold everything he owned so he could buy that property."

Parable 9—The Facts

When I find something valuable, I treasure it. I protect it and make sure no one can take it away from me. God's gift of love is a valuable treasure. It's more important than anything in this world.

1. If you found a hidden treasure, what are the first two things you would do to keep it safe?

   - _____

   - _____

2. What are the two most valuable treasures in your *life*?

   - _____

   - _____

3. If you've chosen friendship with God as a valuable treasure, what two things could destroy it if you're not careful?

   - _____

   - _____

4. If you've chosen health as a valuable treasure, name two things that could destroy it

   - _____

   - _____

5. Whenever you're tempted to destroy one of your treasures, how can God help you preserve it?

   _____

   _____

PARABLE 10

Seeds

MATTHEW 21:33–43

Seeds?"

"Yes."

"You gave me seeds for my birthday?"

Grandpa smiled. "You were born in the spring, so I thought, What better symbol of your spring birth than—?"

"Seeds."

"You got it."

Twelve-year-old Daryl studied the small, brightly-colored packets stacked neatly in his open palm. Each carried a different name: cucumber, squash, red pepper, tomato, spinach, and kale. "They'll make a wonderful salad someday," his grandfather interjected. "Sprinkle a little lemon juice over the top and *mmm, mmm*, good! I'll come back later in the year to enjoy it with you, OK?"

The last thing Daryl wanted to do was show disappointment over his unexpected gift. His grandpa—who lived in a neighboring state—was a skilled gardener. But packets of seeds were also the last thing Daryl wanted for his birthday. He had his heart set on a new skateboard and had been dropping hints large enough to trip over during the past few weeks. But it seemed his efforts were in vain.

No skateboard this year! Just . . . seeds.

"Thank you, Grandpa," the boy said with more enthusiasm than he felt. "I'll be sure to stick them in the ground first chance I get."

"You'd better not put if off too long," Grandpa warned lovingly. "It's planting season right now and the ground is just waiting for you to till it, weed it, and mix in some good ol' organic fertilizer. Oh and be sure to read the instructions on each packet before planting. Then you'll know how deep and how far apart to place the seeds. It'll be a piece of cake—or, should I say, a piece of *salad.*" The man tilted back his head and laughed loudly at his own joke.

"Got it, Grandpa," Daryl said, forcing a chuckle. He admired his grandfather and wanted to make him happy. But seeds? For your twelfth birthday?

True to his word, Daryl got busy just a few days later and stuck the seeds in the ground. Although he'd much rather be doing ollies with a new skateboard, he managed to plant his future salad with a degree of care. His rows were almost straight, and he hoped the depth he'd chosen for each planting—who has time to read instructions?—was enough to satisfy Mother Nature. He watered down the whole patch of earth and prepared to enjoy his summer. Waiting for a garden to grow was about as exciting as watching cement dry.

Every few weeks, a package would arrive from Grandpa. "Thought this would be helpful," said a note taped on the cover of a book entitled, *Caring for Your Summer Garden.* Another bundle included a small bag of some sort of mineral with instructions to "sprinkle this on your squash plants right away." Yet another contained a new hand spade. Daryl mindlessly tossed each new gift in with the others in the basement and went about the business of having fun hanging out with his friends.

His garden, in the meantime, grew and grew. And, because the boy would rather spend time at the local skateboard park instead of seeing to his future salad, so did the weeds.

"How's it going, Daryl?" The boy recognized the voice.

"Hey, Uncle Jason," he called out just as he completed an

awesome kickflip at the park. "What are you doing here?"

The man smiled. "Just thought I'd check in with you. Your grandpa wants to know how your garden is doing. I'd like to take a few pictures to send to him."

Daryl froze. "Ah, well, I'm sorry Uncle Jason. But I don't have time to take you over there right now. I'm kinda busy."

"But your grandpa—"

"Really, Uncle Jason," the boy interrupted, feeling just a bit irritated. "I can't leave now. I'm learning a new trick and I gotta finish my practice. Another time, OK?"

The man shrugged. "OK."

Daryl watched his visitor get into his car and drive away. Actually his garden looked terrible. Half the plants were dead from lack of watering, and the other half were in a life-and-death struggle with weeds. But who wanted a garden anyway? Skateboarding was much more fun! Besides, maybe Grandpa would learn a lesson from all this. The next time his birthday rolled around, there'd be no more seed gifts. No, sir. Maybe a remote-controlled airplane. Yeah. That would be perfect. Grandpa could just give his silly seeds to someone else.

Matthew 21:33–43

Jesus told another story. "A wealthy man owned a vineyard. He put a fence around it, made a winepress, and built a watchtower. Then he rented it out and left on business. When it was time for the harvest, he sent some of his servants to collect his share of the harvest as rent.

"But the renters beat up one, stoned another, and killed another. Then the owner sent some more servants, but the renters treated them the same way.

"Finally the landowner decided to send his own son. He said, 'I know they'll respect my son.' But when they saw the son coming, they said, 'He's the owner's only son. Let's kill him. Then the vineyard will belong to us.' So that's what they did. What do you think the landowner will do to these men?"

The priests answered, "The owner will have the evil renters arrested and tried for murder. Then he'll get other renters to look after his vineyard."

Jesus said, "Haven't you read in the Scriptures how the Temple builders rejected the stone that would fit the corner? The Temple stone and the landowner's son represent Me. If you reject Me, My Father will give His vineyard to people who know how to take care of it.

"I am the Cornerstone. He who accepts Me will feel sorry for his sins, and God will forgive him. But he who does not, God will have to let him die with the wicked."

After listening to these parables, the priests knew that Jesus was talking about their plans to kill Him. They would have arrested Jesus right then, but they were afraid, because the people loved Jesus and believed in Him.

Parable 10—Seeds

God's gifts to me are very important. But if I don't take care of the gifts He has given me, something bad happens. I don't get to enjoy the many benefits of those wonderful gifts. Then I lose both the gift and the joy it would bring.

1. Name three gifts that God gives to every human being on earth:

- _____

- _____

- _____

2. How can we destroy each of these three gifts?

_____

_____

3. How can we save and enjoy each of these three gifts?

_____

_____

4. Is there a special gift that God has given to you?

_____

_____

5. What can you do, starting today, to make sure your special gift is safe and secure, out of the devil's reach and those who would destroy it?

_____

_____

ROI

MATTHEW 25:14–28

O
K. Here's the deal." The man smiled down at his three daughters as he paced back and forth in front of them. The girls stood in a neat row, eyes forward, hands at their sides. "I'm being deployed for six months, and in my absence, I'm expecting you to take good care of your mother and the dog."

"Yes, sir!" the girls chorused, smiles playing at the corners of their lips. They loved their dad very much, even though he tended to be a bit "military" from time to time. But, hey, he was the captain of a powerful Navy aircraft carrier and was used to giving orders and keeping everything "shipshape" as he'd say.

"I'm leaving some important items in your charge," the man continued, studying the faces of his young listeners. "For you, Victoria, I'm giving you control of my new computer. You may use it in any way you see fit."

Fourteen-year-old Victoria grinned broadly. She was the family geek and had been eyeing the new addition to her dad's home office for days. "Yes, sir!" she responded. "Thank you, sir."

"And you, Elizabeth," the man said, eyeing his twelve-year-old— whose skills included climbing trees, running races, and beating boys at baseball, "I'm allowing you unlimited access to my twenty-one-speed bicycle."

"You mean the one with the full carbon clincher, Shimano derailleur, and titanium frame?"

"That's the one."

"Yes, sir!"

"And for you, Sarah, I'm assigning you my brand-new digital camera complete with three lenses, tripod, and flash."

Thirteen-year-old Sarah blinked. "But, sir, that's a very expensive camera."

"Yes it is," Dad agreed. "So use it with care."

"Yes, sir."

The man paused. "Now, the reason I have made these arrangements with you is so that, for the next six months, you can find ways to increase my investments and to make some serious spending money for yourselves. Using the tools I've given you, I want each of you to enjoy a healthy ROI. I'll expect a full report on my return."

"ROI, sir?" Victoria interjected. "What does that mean?"

"It stands for *return on investment*. Every business wants a good return on its investment. That's exactly what I want for you—to make some money to buy things for yourself. Understand?"

"Understood!" the girls chorused.

"One request, sir," Elizabeth stated. "May we hug you goodbye?"

A smile creased the man's face. "Permission granted!"

The three girls threw themselves into their father's arms and kissed his tanned cheeks. How they loved their daddy and how they would miss him while he was gone to sea!

* * * * *

At the end of six months, the girls excitedly stood once again before their father, happy beyond expression that he'd finally returned home.

"And now," the man stated, eyeing each daughter thoughtfully, "you may give me your reports. What was your ROI on the assignments I gave each of you?"

Victoria stepped forward. "I used your computer to set up an eBay account and sold many things that Mom was going to throw away or that no one used anymore. So far I've collected one hundred and thirty-five dollars and have bids on several more items. I'm expecting to add another twenty-five dollars to that amount, sir."

"Excellent!" her daddy enthused. "And you, Elizabeth?"

"Using your bicycle, I got an afternoon job at the fruit market making deliveries to elderly and sick people in town. Adding what the market paid me and tips I received from my happy customers, my ROI comes to sixty-two dollars and eighty-five cents."

"You did a fine job!" the man exclaimed. "And, how about you, Sarah?"

The girl stepped forward. "Daddy, I knew how important—and expensive—that camera is, and I know how angry you'd be if something bad happened to it, so I very carefully put everything in a box and placed it in my closet where nothing would bump into it or bang it around. I took very good care of it and even dusted the box from time to time. So, here it is, safe and sound, just as you left it."

The man's eyes glistened with great disappointment. "Oh Sarah," he said, "you don't understand. The value of what I own is based on what it can do for those I love. If my possessions bring happiness and opportunity to my family, only then are they meaningful to me. That's their worth. That's their ROI."

Matthew 25:14–28

Jesus said, "At the time of the end, it will be like a business owner who went on a long trip. Before he left, he met with his managers and told them what he wanted them to do. He gave one $5,000, another $2,000, and another $1,000, depending on their ability.

"The manager with $5,000 invested it in the business, and soon had $10,000. The one with $2,000 did the same thing, and soon had $4,000. But the one who had $1,000 did nothing with it. He just took it home and buried it.

"After some time the business owner came back and called his managers together to see how things had gone while he was away.

"The first manager said, 'Sir, you gave me $5,000, and I doubled it for you.' The owner said, 'You did well. Now I can trust you with even more.'

"The next one said, 'Sir, you gave me $2,000, and I too doubled it.' The owner said, 'You did well. Now I can trust you with even more.'

"Then the last one said, 'Sir, you gave me $1,000. I knew that if I lost it, you wouldn't be happy. So I kept it safe at home. Here it is. Let me give it back to you.' The owner said, 'You didn't do what I expected you to do. The least you could have done was to give it to those who know how to invest it. Then it would have brought in something extra for me.

" 'I really can't trust you, so I'll give that money to those who know how to use it. Anyone who uses what I have given him will receive more. Anyone who doesn't will lose what he has. So I'm letting you go, no matter how painful it is.' "

Parable 11—ROI

Return on investment. Every businessman or woman understands that important concept. Because I work hard to make something good happen, I want to enjoy the benefits of my hard work.

1. Let's say that God gave me the talent for making music. What three things could I do to grow my talent and enjoy its benefits?

   - _____

   - _____

   - _____

2. What three things could I do to destroy my musical gift from God?

   - _____

   - _____

   - _____

3. God gives us talents that not only benefit us but they benefit others too. How can I use my music talent to bring happiness and comfort to others?

   _____

4. Knowing that God gives everyone at least one talent, how can I encourage others to find and grow their own personal, God-given talent? Should I make fun of them when they try to do something and fail? What should I do?

   _____

5. When Jesus returns, what does He want to find us doing with the talents—even small ones—that He has given to us?

PARABLE 12

Payback

MATTHEW 18:23–35

O rder! Order in the court!" The judge hammered his gavel on his broad, wooden desk and shouted into the chaos that had suddenly erupted. "If I don't have silence, I will clear this courtroom. Everyone will have to leave."

The commotion eased into an uneasy quiet. The plaintiff—twelve-year-old Justin Parker—stood before the judge, chin lifted, looking defiant and just a bit angry.

"So Mr. Parker," the judge stated, leaning forward in his tall, leather chair, "you are telling this court that you approached your friend Jessica who, just two months before, had borrowed money from you with the promise to pay you back, with interest, within sixty days. Is that correct?"

"Yes, Your Honor."

"And when you approached her with your request for payback, she refused?"

"That is exactly what happened, Your Honor."

The judge frowned. "Did this Jessica give a reason for her refusal to return the money she'd borrowed?"

Justin chuckled. "Oh she said something about her father losing his job and her mother being sick, but I didn't believe her."

"And why didn't you believe her?"

"Because, Your Honor, I saw her father just three days before that working at our school, and I noticed her mother at the grocery store and she didn't look sick at all. As a matter of fact, I asked her how she was and she said, 'Today is a good day.' Now I ask you, does that sound like a sick person to you?"

Those gathered in the courtroom began to respond with sarcastic comments and jeers, but the judge called them back to silence. "I will have to agree with you," the man stated, nodding his head. "That does *not* sound like a sick person to me."

"So," Justin continued, "I'm asking the court to order Jessica to pay back what she owes me *immediately*."

With that, the boy returned to his seat and sat down, a satisfied smile creasing his face.

The judge made a few notations, then looked up again. "The court calls Jessica Miller to the stand."

All eyes watched as a twelve-year-old girl with dark brown hair and sad eyes took her place before the gathering. The judge stared at her for a long moment, and then spoke slowly. "You have heard the charge against you?" he asked.

"Yes, Your Honor, I have."

"And you understand why you have been brought here today?"

"Yes, I do."

"Then would you please explain to the court your action in not returning the money you borrowed from Justin Parker?"

"I will try, Your Honor." The girl cleared her throat. "It is true that I borrowed money from Justin," she said. "It is true that I promised to pay it back. But when my dad lost his job and my mother got sick, all of our money had to go for medicine—"

"Let me stop you right there, Jessica," the judge interrupted. "The plantiff states that he saw your dad working and your mother having a good day at the grocery store."

"Yes, sir," the girl agreed. "But my dad wasn't working. He was volunteering without pay at the school while waiting for someone—anyone—to reply to the dozens of résumés he had sent out. And, yes, my mother was having a good day. But the day before, she'd been in great pain, and the day after she had to see the doctor once again."

Jessica glanced over at her accuser. "And if I may add, Your Honor, Justin should understand what it's like to not be able to repay a loan. My father, before he lost his job because of company cut backs, was a loan officer at the local bank. Justin Parker—along with his father—had borrowed money from the bank to buy a new bicycle. When he missed some payments, my dad asked him why. Justin explained that his brother was in trouble and needed money, and the family was helping him out. So my dad arranged for the bank to wait a few months for payments and even lowered the amount owed. That was all I was asking of Justin—to give me more time to repay the money I had borrowed. But he brought me here instead."

The judge thought for a long moment, then looked over at Justin. "Young man, your actions will serve as my judgment. I show mercy only to those who show mercy. Case dismissed!"

Matthew 18:23–35

"God's kingdom is like a king who went to see how his servants were doing. He found that a high official had stolen a huge sum of money from him. And the man had spent it all. Now, in that country, if a man couldn't pay back what he stole, the king would put him in jail, take his property, and sell his family as slaves.

"The man fell on his knees and pleaded, 'Please, give me a chance! I promise you I will pay it back.' The king felt sorry for him and said, 'I forgive you. So forget about what you owe me.'

"Then the official went to see a man who owed him

money. He grabbed him by the throat and demanded that he pay him right away. The man fell on his knees, begged for forgiveness, and promised to pay him back. But the official refused to listen. Instead, he had the man thrown in jail.

"The king's servants heard about it and told the king. The king called in this official. 'You really deserve to be punished,' he said. 'I forgave you all that money you stole, and even gave you back your job. Why didn't you forgive the man who owed you money? Why weren't you as good to him as I was to you?'

"The king was really upset. He had no choice but to throw the man in jail until he or someone else paid all the money he owed. That's what God will have to do to those who don't forgive others."

Parable 12—Payback

I believe that God is a fair God. But sometimes, He's only as fair with us as we are with others. I think He does that to teach us an important lesson.

1. Why does God sometimes treat us like we treat other people?

_____

_____

2. If we want God to forgive us, how should we treat our friends and family? What kind of message am I sending to God when I'm unkind, unforgiving, and unfaithful?

_____

_____

3. Does God forgive me when I make mistakes and am unkind? If He does, how should I treat people who are unkind to me? Give an example.

_____

_____

4. Is there a time limit on God's forgiveness? Will He still forgive me for something I did a long time ago?

_____

_____

5. If God didn't have such a forgiving spirit, would anyone on earth be able to look forward to heaven?

_____

_____

The Invitation

W hat do you mean he's not coming?" Sheriff Jodie Shards looked up from his list and frowned. "He *has* to come. The river is rising, and his house is close to the bank."

Deputy Martin shrugged. "He says he'll be just fine. Told me to tell you—and I quote—'I've seen this river rise and fall all my life, and my house has withstood every storm.' "

Shards shook his head. "That may be true. But this storm is different." He picked up the phone and started dialing then stopped. "Line is dead. Water must've knocked down the poles west of town." He checked his list. "How about the Dowds or the Stewards? Oh and did you happen to see Old Man McClintock? Surely they all recognize a dangerous flood when they see one."

Deputy Martin checked his ever-present notepad. "Mr. Dowd said: 'Nothing to worry about.' " He flipped a page. "Mrs. Steward said, 'Thank you but no thank you.' As for Old Man McClintock, he took a shot at me the minute I walked onto his property. Said he doesn't trust cops and would rather face a flood than hang out with the likes of you or me."

The sheriff let out a frustrated groan. "Most of these people are on my danger list for whenever the river rises. They need to be evacuated. Of course, it's up to them. I can't force them to do anything. If they want to be stubborn and remain in harm's way, that's their choice."

He paused, drumming his fingers on the desk. "What about others in town? Anyone else needing to take refuge here at the station? We're on high ground and the river can't reach us. I've got lots of food and water and bedding. People can sleep in the garage, the equipment room, or even in the empty jail cells if necessary. That's got to be better than floating downstream in the middle of the night."

"I'll ask," the deputy called over his shoulder as he hurried out the door.

An hour later, the police station was packed with people, all trying to escape the rising waters and driving rains that threatened to devastate their small, riverside community. There were men and women, boys and girls, rich families and poor families, even a few new arrivals who had come to town just the summer before, trying to escape dangerous situations in their faraway homelands. They looked lost and confused, even as Deputy Martin tried to reassure them that they were safe from the storm and should feel free to enjoy the nice meal being prepared.

As Sheriff Shards maneuvered through the gathering, he came upon none other than Old Man McClintock looking stern and nervous. In his hands, he clutched his powerful hunting rifle complete with sighting scope, polished metal, and wood surfaces. "Well hello, Joseph," the sheriff said, walking up to him. "Glad you decided to join us. But I have to tell you that—"

"Leave me alone," the old man shot back, his face as fierce as the storm raging outside. "I'm here 'cause my daughter dragged me here. This storm ain't nothin'. I seen worse."

"OK," the sheriff responded. "But, you can't carry that rifle around with you here in the police station—or around town for that matter. Why don't you just let me—"

"Back off," the man said, lowering his weapon slightly. "No one takes my gun. I got a constitutional right, you know."

"You've got a constitutional right to defend yourself," Shards answered, "but no one here is threatening you. All I'm asking is that you give me your rifle for the time being. I'll be happy to return it after—"

"I said *back off*!"

Suddenly, Old Man McClintock found himself on the floor, held there by Deputy Martin and Sheriff Shards. "Sorry, can't do that," the sheriff responded. "Either you surrender your weapon or leave. Your choice."

* * * *

The next morning, residents of the small town wandered through debris-littered streets. Water damage was extensive. Several houses had been washed away by the flood, including Old Man McClintock's cabin by the river. The last anyone ever saw of him was when he'd stormed out of the sheriff's office the night before, clutching his beloved rifle.

Matthew 22:1–14

Jesus told the people another story. "The way God decides who will get to heaven is like a wedding. The king's son was getting married, so the king planned a big wedding.

"He sent his servants to tell those who had been invited to the wedding to come to it, but they weren't willing to come. Then when it was time for the wedding to begin, the king said to his servants, 'Go, tell my invited guests to come quickly, because everything is ready.'

"But some people were too busy buying, selling, and farming. Others actually mistreated the king's servants and, in some cases, killed them. When the king heard about this, he sent his soldiers out to catch those murderers.

"Then he said to his servants, 'The banquet is ready, but those who don't want to come don't deserve to be here. Go out and invite anyone you see to come and celebrate my son's wedding with me.' So the servants went out and invited everyone they could. Soon the place was full.

"Then the king came in to welcome the guests, and to make sure everyone was wearing the special clothes he had provided. One man was wearing his own everyday clothes. The king said to him, 'Friend, how did you get in here without wearing wedding clothes?' The man didn't know what to say, because he had no excuse.

"Then the king said to his servants, 'Take this man to the door and tell him to leave.' The man cried and begged, but it was no use. Many are invited to the wedding of God's Son, but some are asked to leave because they're not wearing the wedding clothes He provided."

Parable 13—The Invitation

The Bible tells me that God wants *everyone* saved. He wants *everyone* to live with Him in heaven. If someone isn't there, it's because they refused God's loving invitation!

1. What are three ways that God invites each one of us to live with Him in heaven?

   - _____
   - _____
   - _____

2. How do people ignore the three ways you listed above?

   - _____
   - _____
   - _____

3. What is keeping so many people from accepting the invitation to live in heaven someday? Do they not know what heaven is, or do they just not care?

   _____

   _____

4. How can we all help people develop a desire to live with God in heaven forever?

   _____

   _____

5. What can we do each day to keep our excitement about our heavenly home alive and growing?

PARABLE 14

Fashion Sense

MATTHEW 6:28–30

ow! Who are you wearing?" Lorelei gushed as Emily walked up to her in the crowded high school hallway.

"What do you mean, 'Who am I wearing?' " Emily asked.

"You know," Lorelei pressed. "That's what they say at Hollywood awards shows. Who are you wearing? Prada? Versace? Armani? In other words, which famous designer created your new outfit, which, I might add, looks fabulous on you! So let me ask again. Who are you wearing?"

"Walmart."

Lorelei frowned. "You have no fashion sense at all," she moaned. "You could at least have bought something with a label."

"This has a label," Emily countered. "Right here on the jacket. See? It says 'Medium.' "

Lorelei closed her eyes and sighed. "Of all the people in this school I could have chosen to be my best friend, I would have to choose you. You're absolutely bad for my image."

Emily closed her locker door and the two friends started toward the cafeteria. "Tell you what," she said. "The next time I buy clothes, I'll try to get something with some foreign guy's name on it. But only if it's in my mom and dad's price range. Dad is between jobs and Mom is working two shifts at a restaurant. Our clothes budget may not be big enough to include some guy who's famous enough to have his name stamped on his clothes."

Lorelei adjusted the lapel of her jacket so it lay just so. "But, aren't you even the least bit jealous of people who wear designer fashions?"

"Nope," Emily responded. "I'm just glad I don't have to walk around wearing a garbage bag with cutouts for my arms and head. I figure God has enough to worry about."

"God?" her friend questioned. "What's He got to do with fashion?"

"Well, the flowers of the field look pretty awesome," Emily said with a smile. "You know—lilies, roses, dandelions, and those little blue things that grow beside our driveway at home. Not a label in sight. They bloom, stick around for a few days, and then just wither away. So I figure if God wanted me to wear some Italian guy's clothes, I would. But, He seems to be perfectly happy with me wearing whatever my parents can afford. Who am I to argue with God?"

Lorelei was silent as the two moved through the serving line. Emily chose her usual fare—French fries, baked beans, spinach, and a fruit salad. Her friend did the same—but added a slice of rye bread and a cup of mixed nuts. Just as they were seating themselves at their usual table by the window, Terrilee Webster approached, her nose held in its usual, slightly tilted-up position.

"Well, well," she said, loud enough for most in the room to hear, "looks as if Emily got herself a new outfit. Isn't that special! I'd buy myself something new, but my closet is just too jammed with clothes from the finest stores in our town—or any town for that matter. If a designer made it, I've got it."

She bent down to examine Emily's jacket and blouse. "Hmm. You're going to have to help me here. I can't seem to see any name. Surely you didn't purchase something—I shudder to even say it—'off the rack' where just anyone can buy it. I mean, who wants to look like everyone else in town? I sure don't. So Emily my dear, you're going to have to tell me. Who are you wearing?"

Lorelei slowly rose to her feet and positioned herself between her friend and Terrilee. "I can answer that," she said with a smile. "My friend Emily is wearing something created for her by the most famous Designer in the universe."

"Really?" Terrilee gasped, trying to look surprised. "And who might that be?"

"I admire your fashion sense, Terrilee," Lorelei responded. "You certainly know a great design when you see it, and so does my best friend Emily. I'm very proud to say that she is wearing the best designer—God."

Matthew 6:28–30

"Why worry so much about clothes? Look at how beautiful the flowers are. Do they sew and work at looking good? Yet they are more beautiful than a king in all his fine clothes. Now, if God is interested in flowers that live only a short time, how much more is He interested in you?"

Parable 14—Fashion Sense

God takes care of me. How do I know this? Because today I had something to eat, something to wear, and something to do. The devil wants me starving, naked, and lazy.

1. What is your favorite fruit (apples, oranges, mangoes, etc.)? What is your favorite vegetable (squash, carrots, broccoli, etc.)? What is your favorite whole grain (wheat, barley, oats, etc.)? You just named three gifts from God!

   _____

2. Finish these sentences with your own words:

   • God gives me beautiful things to see, hear, taste, smell, and eat because _____.

   • I know these gifts are from God because the devil wants me to _____.

3. Even though the flowers of the field look beautiful and make us happy, does God (1) completely shield them from heavy rains, damaging winds, or hurtful hail, or does He (2) make them strong and able to withstand the most violent weather?

   _____

4. For a flower to be beautiful and smell sweet, it needs _____. For me to offer a beautiful Christian service to the world and make people happy, I need _____.

5. The most important thing for me to do to share God's love is to (1) make a lot of money, (2) put myself first in everything, or (3) demonstrate Jesus' love to others by the way I act, what I say, and how I treat them.

Henry's Heart

MATTHEW 5:13

enry sighed the type of sigh that thirteen-year-old boys share with the world when they're feeling totally bored and wish they were somewhere other than where they are. He looked around the crowded room and frowned. Homeless people. What was wrong with them? Why didn't they just get jobs so they could buy their own food, fix it in their own kitchens, and eat it in their own dining rooms?

But, no. They'd rather ruin his Wednesday evening and show up here at the soup kitchen like a bunch of hungry sheep eager to gobble down his mother's vegetable stew, whole wheat bread, and fresh peaches, which—he reminded himself—he'd picked in the hot sun from the small orchard beside their house that very afternoon. He and his mom had done all the work. Now these people were enjoying the fruits of their labor without even having to break a sweat.

"Hey sweetie," his mother called as she hurried by, arms filled with bunches of colorful carrots—another gift from their property— "would you give me a hand? There are some beets in the car and I need that new bag of salt brought in as well. Make it snappy. We've got hungry mouths to feed."

Henry shrugged and headed for the door, weaving his way around tables crowded with patiently waiting diners. At first, he'd enjoyed working with his mother at the community soup kitchen. But lately, it had become just another item on his growing list of things he didn't want to do with his valuable time. He'd much rather play soccer with the guys or be on social media.

As he reached the car parked by the curb, a mother and her young son hurried by, headed for the entrance to the soup kitchen. The boy—Henry figured him to be around eight years old—suddenly stopped. "I don't want to go in there," he said, chin jutting out slightly.

His mother turned to face him. "Now Toby, we've talked about this."

"I know, but I don't want to. The kids at school make fun of me because we eat here twice a week. They call me names and say Daddy is a loser."

"Your daddy is *not* a loser!" the mother countered firmly. "He lost his job and can't find work. So we have to eat here. You want to go hungry?"

"No."

"Then let's get inside before they run out of food. We don't have much left in the car. When your father gets back from the city, we'll figure something out. Might even get an apartment or something. Until then we have to depend on these nice people to help us."

The boy's shoulders sagged just a little. "Will we always be poor?"

"No," his mother said softly. "God will take care of us. God will provide. You'll see."

The two continued toward the entrance of the soup kitchen. Henry watched them go as he stood beside the car, trying to imagine what it would be like to have so little that you were forced to depend on the kindness of strangers.

Then it hit him. He was supposed to be one of those strangers. He was supposed to be the hope that people like that mother and little son desperately needed as they struggled with life. He realized that his heart had become cold and uncaring because he had forgotten why he was doing what he was doing and why his mother worked so hard to provide a tasty meal for the needy people of their town.

Something changed in him at that moment; something deep inside. If he was to be that stranger, if he was to be that hope—he wanted to do it with a thankful heart.

Henry reached into the back seat and grabbed a colorful collection of beets and the small bag of salt. He also selected the biggest, juiciest peach from the basket and jammed it into his jacket pocket. He knew that a certain little boy would appreciate the fruit's sweetness. And for the first time in weeks, Henry knew he'd serve those waiting in the soup kitchen with a genuine and heartfelt smile on his face.

Matthew 5:13

Jesus went on to say, "You are like salt. But if salt loses its salty taste, it can't make food taste good or keep it from spoiling. It's good for nothing. People throw it away."

Parable 15—Henry's Heart

I want to taste good to the world. No, I'm not saying anyone is going to eat me. But God says I'm supposed to add "flavor" to the lives of the people I meet, just like salt adds flavor to my favorite vegetables.

1. How would you describe the taste of something that "needs salt"?

_____

_____

2. How would you describe a person who only thinks of himself or herself and ignores everyone else?

_____

_____

3. How did Jesus add "flavor" to the lives of the following men?

   • Zacchaeus the tax collector sitting up in the tree

   • Peter the disciple who told everyone, "I don't know Jesus"

   • The thief on the cross dying beside Him on Calvary

4. How can we add "flavor" to the life of someone who is

   • Sad? _____

   • Afraid? _____

   • Angry? _____

5. In what ways does God add "flavor" to your life every day?

_____

_____

PARABLE 16

Pop Quiz

MATTHEW 24:42–51

S cotty squinted through the bright afternoon sunlight and studied the batter poised at home plate. "You're going down," he called out, trying to sound menacing, although his opponent just happened to be his best friend Tony.

"In your dreams," Tony shot back. "I can hit anything you can throw."

"Yes, but can you name the three states of water?"

Tony blinked. "What?"

"Can you name the three states of water?" the pitcher repeated.

The batter lowered his bat. "What are you talking about?"

Scotty remained in windup position, ready to hurl the softball toward home plate. "Mrs. Tucker said there might be a pop quiz in science class tomorrow and I just wanted to make sure we're all ready for it."

"Solid, liquid, and gas," the first baseman shouted. "Now throw the ball!"

"Very good," Scotty responded as he sent the white sphere curving toward Tony. "But do you know the chemical formula for water?"

With a resounding *plat*, the ball slammed into the catcher's mitt. "Aren't we supposed to be playing softball instead of playing school?" his teammate shouted as he tossed the ball back toward the pitcher's mound.

"Chemical formula?" Scotty called out again. "Anybody?"

"Two hydrogen atoms to one oxygen atom," the left outfielder yelled, sounding a bit frustrated. "Everybody knows that."

"I didn't know that," the shortstop chimed in, rubbing his chin with the tip of his glove. "When did Mrs. Tucker teach us that?"

"Must have been during your usual ten-thirty nap," the catcher chided with a chuckle. "Last year you missed the entire Vietnam War the same way."

"Hey, science and history make me sleepy," the shortstop countered.

Scotty squinted again, studying Tony's posture, looking for a weak spot that would affect his swing. That's where he'd place the ball. "At sea level," he called out, "at what temperature does water boil?"

"Enough with the science review, Scotty," Tony moaned. "Just throw the ball!"

Scotty nodded. "Hey," he said, beginning his carefully choreographed windup. "Softball won't get me into college. Knowing at what temperature water boils may."

"Two hundred and twelve degrees Fahrenheit," the right outfielder shouted. He paused. "Speaking of water, anyone else thirsty?"

Scotty sent the ball slicing through the air straight at the pitcher's outstretched glove. Tony blurred the bat, hitting the fast-moving sphere with a satisfying *thwat*, arching it towards center field. "Good hit!" teammates yelled from the bench.

"Good catch!" other voices chimed in two seconds later.

"You distracted me with all your water talk," Tony groaned as he and Scotty passed each other, one on the way to right field, the other heading in the direction of the benches. "And what's with all this science garbage? We're here to enjoy ourselves, not learn something."

"Ah, come on, Tony," Scotty pressed. "There really might be a pop quiz tomorrow, and I know that science isn't exactly your best subject. After all Mrs. Tucker refers to you as her 'greatest challenge.' I just want you to get a good grade and—"

"Might be, *might be* a pop quiz, right?" Tony interrupted. "So there's a fifty-fifty chance that there will *not* be a pop quiz tomorrow. Why on earth should I study for something that might not even happen?"

"Well," the pitcher countered, "if it's not tomorrow, it'll be someday. We need to be prepared."

"Fine," Tony shrugged. "You prepare. I'll play ball."

Scotty sighed as he watched his friend walk away. There was nothing else he could do. "Water is a good sound conductor," he called after him. "Sonar? Depth recorders? Remember?"

Tony motioned as if swatting away a mosquito. Then he took up his position ready to continue the after-school game.

The next morning, Mrs. Tucker announced to the science class, "There will now be a pop quiz. The subject? Water!"

Scotty glanced over at Tony who closed his eyes and dropped his head into his hands. The teacher lifted the map of the world covering the questions on the whiteboard as Scotty grabbed his pencil. Maybe his best friend would know some of the answers—at least enough of them to pass the test.

Matthew 24:42–51

"Those who love Me will have to keep watching, because no one knows the exact time when I'll come back. If a man knew when a thief would break into his house, he would stay awake and watch for him. That's what My people need to do, because when they least expect it, that's when I'll come.

"The way to be ready is to be like a good servant. He

takes care of his master's things and helps his fellow servants while his master is away. The master will be very happy when he returns, because his servant did a good job in looking after things. He'll promote that servant and trust him with everything he has.

"People who don't put the things of God first are like a servant who thinks that his master will be gone a long time. He doesn't take care of his master's things and doesn't help his fellow servants. He thinks only about himself.

"But when he's not expecting it, suddenly his master will return and surprise him. He will dismiss that servant to join others like him. That servant will not only lose his job, but will suffer even more than you can imagine."

Parable 16—Pop Quiz

Have you ever been surprised? I sure have. Sometimes it's fun. Sometimes it's not. But I always learn something!

1. Name three situations that you would consider to be happy surprises.

   - _____
   - _____
   - _____

2. Name three situations that you would consider unhappy surprises.

   - _____
   - _____
   - _____

3. What makes a surprise happy?

   _____

   _____

4. What makes a surprise unhappy?

   _____

   _____

5. We will always face unhappiness in this sinful world, but what can we do to be happy?

   _____

   _____

Sandy's Secret

MATTHEW 11:16–19

L ook at her," Deanne sneered, whispering behind her hand as she leaned toward Rosemary's desk. "She can't even keep her eyes open for more than a minute. Her head drops down and then snaps back up. Must be on drugs or something."

Rosemary frowned. She'd noticed her classmate's struggle to pay attention in English class for the past few weeks but had never worked up enough courage to ask why. Eighth-grade English was tough enough when you were wide awake. She couldn't even imagine—

"Time's up," the teacher called from his desk. "Please pass your essays to your left and I'll collect them. Class dismissed."

As the students filed out of the room, Rosemary could overhear others talking in low tones about Sandy's lack of attention. "She's lazy," she heard one say. "Total goof-off," another chimed in. "She's going to fail this class for sure," yet another interjected just loud enough for Sandy to hear.

Rosemary glanced in Sandy's direction. The girl remained seated, staring at her textbook. A single tear slipped from her eye and formed a tiny, moist streak down her cheek. Yet, she said nothing. Not one word.

Sandy had always been a strange sort of person as far as Rosemary was concerned. Being neighbors, Rosemary would often see her out in her yard tending to the half-dead flowers near her mailbox. As far as she could remember, she'd never seen Sandy smile or say more than five words at a time. She kept to herself, which only added to the mystery surrounding her. But this struggling to pay attention in class was relatively new. Maybe she *was* on drugs. Maybe she *was* lazy. Maybe her classmates were right.

That evening, as Rosemary was enjoying her usual stroll around the neighborhood—a habit she'd picked up after a health and fitness class the year before—she paused in front of Sandy's house. Perhaps the girl needed some sort of help. But she didn't want to intrude. Yet as a Christian, Rosemary knew that she should at least find out.

A weak voice answered her knock. "Come in."

Rosemary entered the house and immediately noticed the unmistakable odor of lavender. She saw a hospital bed set up in the living room by the window and a middle-age woman lying under clean sheets. "Hello there," the woman called. "And who might you be?"

"Hi," Rosemary responded, a bit nervous. "I'm Rosemary. I live just down the street."

"Oh," the woman said with a tired smile. "You must be a friend of my daughter, Sandy."

"Yes," Rosemary nodded. "We attend the same school."

"Well come on in and make yourself comfortable," the woman in the bed invited. "Sandy is not here right now. Had to go to the store to buy a few things for supper. Should be back soon."

Rosemary sat down quietly on the old sofa across the room and looked at her hands, not knowing what else to say.

"My Sandy is something, isn't she?" the woman stated with some effort. Rosemary could tell she was in pain. "She takes such good care of me. It's just her and me, you know. I got heart disease kinda bad. It was touch and go there for a while. But my Sandy stayed by my side constantly. Yes she did. She got me through the operation at county hospital, and now she's my very own nurse here at home. Rubs lavender oil on my aching muscles, fixes my meals, and helps me get through the nights. Don't know what I'd do without her."

Rosemary thought for a long moment, and then stood to her feet. "I need to go home and get something. But I'll be right back," she announced. "I've got some notes from English class today and was wondering if Sandy would like to go over them with me."

"No problem," the sick woman said with a smile. "My Sandy's always been a straight A student and I'm sure she'd appreciate the company. She doesn't get out much 'cause of me. I know she'd love to study English with you. It's her favorite subject." The woman paused. "She's my angel, you know. My precious angel."

Matthew 11:16–19

"People today are like two groups of children playing games. One group says to the other, 'Nothing we play pleases you, whether we play happy songs or sad songs.'

"John preached a strong message, and some said it was too strong. Then I come along, and they say that I'm not strict enough because I forgive sins. People are wise enough to know the difference between what's right and what isn't."

Parable 17—Sandy's Secret

Sometimes life can frustrate you. Have you ever had someone think something about you that wasn't true? It has certainly happened to me. It happened—and is still happening—to God.

1. When Jesus came to this world, God's people were expecting a warrior King—Someone who would defeat their enemies and rule over the land. But what did they get? How would you describe Jesus?

   _____

2. Which is more important: (1) What someone says or (2) what someone does?

   _____

   _____

3. Which is more important: (1) What someone says someone does or (2) what you've seen that person do?

   _____

   _____

4. You've heard the saying, "Walk the talk"? That means a person does what he or she says. I want to walk my talk. Should I: (1) work hard to do whatever I say or (2) work hard to make sure that whatever I say I can do—or at least be willing to learn how to do it?

   _____

   _____

5. Did Jesus walk the talk? What story about Him demonstrates to you that He did exactly what He said He would do?

   _____

Patches

LUKE 15:11–32

Will he ever come back?" Toby asked as he sat on the front porch looking out across the lawn toward the tree-lined street. "It's been a month and I miss him."

"Hard to tell," his father said with a sigh. "Dogs sometimes do strange things, such as run away from a perfectly good home. It's the 'call of the wild' I guess."

"I did give him a good home, didn't I?" the boy asked, his voice trembling slightly. "I mean, I fed him lots of his favorite food, played with him each day after school, and even let him sleep on my bed—on my pillow! He'd curl up in a little ball and snore right in my ear." Toby paused as sudden tears stung his eyes. "I thought he liked living here with me. I thought he was happy."

"I'm sure he was," Father said, slipping an arm around his son. "But dogs are wild creatures at heart. There's something deep inside of them that can sometimes lure them away from home—away from young boys who care for them and love them."

Toby nodded slowly. "Well, I'm not going to give up. No, sir. I'm going to take my bicycle and ride around the neighborhood each and every day. Maybe he'll see me and notice how sad I am without him. Maybe he'll hear me calling and want to come home."

"You never know," his father said, rising to his feet. "Anything is possible." With that, he walked into the house as Toby hurried in the direction of the garage.

"Patches. *Paaaatchessss.*" The mournful call of a young boy riding his bicycle slowly along Hillcrest Drive echoed among the homes and gardens of the cozy subdivision. The neighbors had heard it before and stopped whatever they were doing to wave encouragement as the rider drifted by. There was such heartbreak in that voice that each hearer hoped tonight would be the night that the missing dog would finally return. But after so many evenings of listening to that call, they were beginning to lose hope. Patches seemed to have moved on for good.

After an hour of fruitless searching, Toby noticed that the street lamps were beginning to blink on, a signal, designated by his parents, that it was time for little boys on bicycles to come straight home.

He coasted up the driveway and parked his trusty bike next to the car in the garage. Before he went inside for the night, he stood on the front porch and studied the shadows of the evening. Where was Patches? Why was he gone? Was he OK? Was he hurt? Would he ever come back?

Turning toward the front door, the boy suddenly stiffened. What was that? A whimper? A bark? He spun around. There, in the distance, far down the street, stumbling in the gathering darkness was a familiar form. "Patches," the boy whispered. Then he screamed, "PATCHES!"

The dog must have heard his name because he quickened his pace. But the pains of malnourishment and the results of encounters with angry animals twice his size kept him limping along at a frustratingly slow pace. Down the street, he saw a boy running in his direction. Not just any boy. *His* boy. His Toby!

Suddenly he found himself being lifted by gentle arms and soothed by a voice he'd been missing with all his heart. The wild—that great adventure beyond the yard; that call of mysteries unknown—had carried him away from those arms and comforting voice. But he'd soon learned that there were dangers waiting out there along with endless hunger and frightening loneliness. Not every boy was gentle. Not every yard was safe. He'd been away so long that he wasn't even sure if he'd be welcomed back to the yard he loved or accepted by the boy on whose pillow he longed to sleep.

But, now he knew. The face he'd rejected was illuminated by a warm, welcoming smile.

He'd come home, unsure of what he'd find. To his amazement, he quickly realized that all he'd left was still waiting for him. The wild offered nothing but pain and danger. Here in the boy's arms, he knew he'd found all he'd ever need in the whole wide world.

Luke 15:11–32

Then Jesus told another story. "There was a man who had two sons. The younger one wanted to leave home. So he said to his father, 'Father, let me have my inheritance now while I'm still young and can enjoy it.' Reluctantly the father gave him his share of the family money.

"A few days later the son left and went to another country, where he spent his money having a good time. Before long it was all gone. Then some tough times came to that country, and he couldn't find a job.

"Finally a man hired him to take care of his pigs. He didn't want the job, but had no choice. He got so hungry that even what the pigs ate looked good. But no one offered to feed him.

"Then he came to his senses and said, 'What am I doing here? My father has lots of people working for him, and they're all well paid. There's so much food that they throw the leftovers away! And here I am sitting on the ground starving to death!

" 'I'll go back home and say to my father, "Father, please forgive me for what I've done. I have sinned against you and God. I'm not fit to be your son. But please let me work for you like a servant" '

"As weak as he was, he headed for home. But while he was still a long way off, his father spotted him. His heart went out to his son, and he ran to meet him. He threw his arms around him, hugged him, and kissed him, and they both cried.

"When the boy got control of himself, he said, 'Father, please forgive me. I have sinned against you and God. I'm not fit to be called your son . . .'

"The father interrupted him by calling the servants, who came running: 'Quick, go back to the house and get my best robe, the family ring, and some sandals for my son.

" 'Then get the best calf we have, slaughter it, and prepare a banquet. It's time to celebrate. I thought that my son was dead, but he's alive! And he's home. He was lost, but is found.' The servants did so, and soon everyone was celebrating.

"The father's older son had been working in the field. When he came close to the house and heard music, he asked one of the servants, 'What's going on here?'

"The servant answered, 'Your brother is back! Your father was so happy to see him that he ordered a banquet to celebrate his homecoming.'

"The older brother was so angry that he refused to come to the banquet. So his father went looking for him. When he found him, he asked him to come and join the celebration.

"But he refused and said to his father, 'All these years while my brother was gone spending the family money and having a good time, I was working hard to keep the family farm going. I did what you asked me to do. Yet you never offered to have a big party for me and my friends.

" 'But as soon as this sinning son of yours comes home, having spent his share of the family's money, you have a feast for him!'

"The father answered, 'Son, the whole farm is yours. Your brother has nothing. We're the only ones who care about him. So let's be glad that he's home. I thought that he was dead, but he's alive. Don't you think that's reason enough to celebrate?' "

Parable 18—Patches

Have you ever tried to run away from God? Most people have. But if they're like me, they have discovered that being with God is a whole lot better than being without Him. It's a scary world out there. We need a friend and God wants to be our wonderful, loving Friend.

1. In what ways does a person run away from God?

   _____

   _____

2. You've heard the saying, "The grass is always greener on the other side of the fence." In other words, "Over there is better than here." Is this always true?

   _____

   _____

3. What does the devil do to make "the other side of the fence" so appealing to us?

   _____

   _____

4. What are two things we can do to make our "side of the fence" satisfying even though the devil wants us to wander away to his side of the fence?

   • _____

   • _____

5. Which do you believe will bring us the most happiness? Being where God is or being where the devil is? Why?

   _____

   _____

The Missing State

LUKE 15:8–10

Nebraska is missing," nine-year-old Amy declared as she burst into her older sister's bedroom. "I looked and it was gone. Just *gone*!"

"The authorities in Omaha need to be notified," Katie responded, grabbing her cell phone and starting to enter numbers. Then she paused. "Wait. It's Nebraska. No one will miss it."

Amy flopped down on the bed. "Stop making jokes, Katie," she urged. "This is serious. I have all the other state souvenir spoons from our trip to California three years ago. But now one is missing, and I don't know where it is."

"Nebraska?"

"Yes. Who would want to steal it?"

Katie frowned. "Let me get this straight. You think someone broke into your room, looked around for something to take, bypassed your laptop, smartphone, digital camera, and half-filled piggy bank and made off with a cheap, tourist souvenir that cost, what, ten bucks?"

"It cost eight dollars, and that's not the point," Amy countered. "That spoon is part of a collection of ten and each one is important to me. Besides, I liked Nebraska. It was . . . was . . . flat. And that spoon had a drawing of a cow on it. A *Nebraska* cow. You can't get that just anywhere, you know."

"What's going on?" Dad asked as he stuck his head through the doorway. "Did I hear someone say something's been stolen?"

"Nebraska," Amy stated.

"Have you notified Omaha?" Dad wanted to know.

Amy rolled her eyes. "Will you guys stop joking around? Without Nebraska, my collection isn't complete. Besides I like looking at them and remembering each state that we visited. Iowa, Colorado, Wyoming, Idaho, Oregon, California, they're all important to me. When I see my silver spoons, I pretend that we're driving through that state again, enjoying the view and hearing all the sounds and seeing all the sights. It's something we did together and it was fun."

Dad sat down beside his younger daughter and slipped an arm around her sagging shoulders. "It was fun, wasn't it?" he comforted. "And Nebraska was very . . . very . . . "

"I think *flat* is the word you're searching for," Katie interjected.

"Yes, flat," the man nodded. "But as I remember, it was also where we saw the cow with the broken horn. Amy got very concerned about him, worried that the other cows would laugh at him and call him names like 'Mr. One Horn' or something like that, right?"

Amy brushed hair from her eyes. "He looked sad," she said with a sigh.

"So although that spoon doesn't mean much to everyone else, it means a lot to Amy," Dad continued. "That's why I think we should help her find Nebraska."

"Really?" the young girl enthused. "You'll help me look for it?"

"Absolutely," her father responded. "Now where were you the last time you saw Nebraska?"

"Driving into Colorado on the way to Denver," Katie declared.

"Katherine," Father warned, "let's get serious and help your sister. We want her collection to be complete *right*?"

"Right," Katie nodded. "Sorry, Amy. No more jokes."

The young girl thought for a moment. "I was cleaning the spoons in my bathroom. They tend to get a little dusty hanging up there in their frame above my dresser. I remember that Nevada had a nasty stain on it. I think a bug pooped on it."

Katie opened her mouth to say something, but Dad stopped her. "OK," he urged, looking at Amy. "And you've searched all around your bathroom?"

"Yes. All the states were in the frame when I hung it back on the wall."

"Above your dresser?"

"Right."

"Follow me."

Dad led the two girls into Amy's room and carefully pulled the dresser away from the wall. Amy looked behind it and broke into a big smile. "Nebraska! We found Nebraska!" The girl reached down and retrieved the missing spoon. "Yup, there's the cow and everything!"

Quickly the lost item was returned to the collection and the three stood admiring the spoons' gleaming surfaces and colorful images. They each took a moment to remember what it was like to visit the states represented.

After Dad and Katie left, Amy smiled up at her precious collection. "Now we're all together again," she said with a sigh. Looking straight at Nebraska, she added, "You were lost, but now you're found. Welcome home, Mr. One Horn."

Luke 15:8–10

"It's the same way with a woman who has ten valuable coins, but loses one of them. What does she do? She cleans house looking for the coin until she finds it.

"When she does, she tells her neighbors and friends what happened, and they're all happy with her. That's how it is in heaven. The angels are very happy when someone who was lost turns to God."

Parable 19—The Missing State

Are you important? I am! I'm so important that God died for me. He died for you too. So let me ask you again. Are you important?

1. What makes us important to God? Is it because we're so good, or is it because we're so bad at being good? Did God die for good people or bad people—or both?

   _____

   _____

2. What's the most important item—the thing you love the most—in your bedroom other than your bed, dresser, and desk?

   _____

   _____

3. How would you feel if that item was taken away or went missing?

   _____

   _____

4. Where would you look for it and how long would you look for it?

   _____

   _____

5. How would you feel when you found it? That's how God feels when we allow Him to "find" us in this world of sin.

   _____

   _____

PARABLE 20

Sam's Stash

LUKE 12:15–21

Sam stood and surveyed the contents of his closet with a frown creasing his young face. This just wouldn't do. Something needed to change, fast!

"Hey, Dad," the boy called out as he entered the den where his father was scanning the news headlines on his iPad. "I've got a problem."

"Shoot," the man responded, not looking up from his device.

Sam sighed as he sank onto the couch. "I need more room. I'm maxed out."

"What do you mean 'maxed out'?" His father questioned. "You have a big bedroom. I went in there once and got lost. Had to call 9-1-1."

Sam grinned at his father's attempt at humor. "I'm serious," he stated. "My closet is full of clothes. My dresser drawers are packed. My desk is overflowing. Even under my bed is jammed with storage containers. I don't know what to do."

The man shook his head. "You don't have a *too-small-room* problem. You have a *too-much-stuff* problem."

"No, no, no," Sam asserted. "My stuff is important. Every item is part of who I am."

102

"You're part basketball?" his father asked. "I saw that you had four of them when I was trying to find my way back to civilization."

"And I have six soccer balls and three tennis rackets, but that's not the point. You never know when you might need those things. Same with my collection of pet toys."

The man nodded thoughtfully. "Well, I could see the need for pet toys—if we had a pet."

"Just planning ahead, Dad. Just planning ahead."

Sam's father set aside his iPad and studied his son for a long moment. "So," he said slowly, "if I were to give you, say, the shed for your stuff, would that be enough?"

Sam brightened. "And maybe a corner of the garage too? Yeah. That would do it, at least for a while. I like owning things. I work hard mowing lawns and doing chores to earn the money to buy stuff. Makes me feel important, successful—like Bill Gates."

"I want to show you something," Dad said, rising and motioning toward the front door. "I think I may have the answer to your storage problems."

The boy grinned. *Finally*, he thought, *my dear old dad has seen the light. No more jam-packed room. No more crowded closet. Now I'll have space to grow and expand my empire of valuable treasures!*

After a short minivan ride, the two pulled up in front of a small, unassuming home on the outskirts of town. "Will this do?" Dad asked.

Sam frowned. "What's going on? Why are we here?"

The front door opened and a man and two boys about Sam's age peered into the afternoon sunshine. Sam's father opened the van door and waved. "Hey, Mr. Haddad," he called out. "Just thought we'd stop by to see how you guys are doing."

"Welcome, welcome," the man responded with a thick, Middle Eastern accent. "You are first visitor from church. Please come." Sam and his dad walked up onto the small, somewhat rickety porch. "Everything fine," the man continued with a smile. "It not Syria, but it will do."

"You're from Syria?" Sam asked.

"Yes. We lived near Damascus. But we had to leave when terrorists came."

The group entered the home and Sam immediately realized that the house was in need of much more than a good paint job. It needed furniture too. "We sleep on floor," the man said. "But we don't have to worry about someone dropping bomb on us. Sleep very well."

Sam stood looking at the scene and into the faces of the young boys waiting by their father. They had nothing. Nothing at all!

"Where's your wife?" he asked.

The Syrian man's face shadowed with sadness. "She die on boat," he stated quietly. "But she would like this new home. She would make curtains." The speaker paused as tears suddenly stung his eyes.

Sam thought for a long moment. Then he brightened. "We have to go," he said, "but we'll be right back." Turning to the boys, he asked, "Do you guys like basketball?"

Luke 12:15–21

"Let Me tell you a story: A rich man had a large farm, and every year he had large harvests. It wasn't long before he didn't know where to store it all. He thought about it and said, 'I know! I'll just build bigger barns. Then I'll retire, take it easy, and have a good time.'

"God was sorry that the man didn't think about heaven, because that night he died and left all his money for others to enjoy. That's how it is with those who think only of this life and not about the next one."

Parable 20—Sam's Stash

There are two kinds of treasures—those which will last forever, and those which will not. If I'm going to be a treasure hunter, I think I know which kinds of treasures I should be hunting for.

1. Look around your house and school. What do you see there that you can take with you to heaven?

   _____

2. What three things do you notice that most people are trying to collect and store?

   • _____

   • _____

   • _____

3. If they were hunting treasures that would last forever, what would they be trying to collect and store today?

   • _____

   • _____

   • _____

4. Having earthly treasures (such as smartphones and skateboards and cool clothes) isn't wrong or bad. They're just not practical. But they can serve an important purpose. What can you do with your earthly treasures that will make them more valuable to God?

   _____

5. After we—with God's help—meet our daily needs (such as food, shelter, and education), where's the best place to "store" our treasures where they'll do the most good for everyone?

   _____

Two Masters

LUKE 16:1–13

Emma smiled inwardly as Stacy lobbed praise after praise in her direction. "You got in and out without anyone seeing you," the girl intoned almost breathlessly. "You're a genius! How were you able to get past Mrs. Kellor?"

"Oh it was nothing," Emma said shyly. "I knew she always went for her break at two fifteen sharp. It's the same everyday. So I just hung around outside her office until she left, then went in and got those silly old files."

"Silly old files?" Stacy gasped. "Just the complete set of seventh-grade science tests for the second half of the school year. We got them copied last night, and now it's up to you to sneak the originals back in the file drawer before anyone knows they're missing."

"No problem," Emma said, taking the large, somewhat worn envelope from her friend's outstretched hands. "Two fifteen. Like clockwork. I'll be ready outside her office door. Be in and out before she has time to pour cream in her decaf."

"My hero," Stacy said with a sly grin. "And I'll have your money waiting for you just like I promised. Kids have been lining up to buy copies of those tests. We're raking in big bucks—thanks to you." The girl smiled broadly. "Stacy and Emma. What a team! We're going to go far in this world. You'll see."

With that, the girl hurried away, waving cheerily at passing teachers in the hallway. The instructors smiled and waved back, surprised that a student would take the time to acknowledge their existence outside of the classroom.

Emma shook her head. How could she be so lucky? How could she be so fortunate to have Stacy Carol—the most popular girl in the seventh grade—choose her to hang out with and to take part in her undercover escapades? Yes, she was one fortunate—and soon to be richer—girl. All she had to do now was put the test masters back in Mrs. Kellor's office. In and out, just like before.

Sure enough, at precisely 2:15 P.M., the science teacher walked out the door, favorite mug in hand, and headed down the hallway, maneuvering around the flow of students going from classroom to classroom. Quickly, Emma slipped into the now empty office, closed the door behind her, and made her way to the file cabinet by the window. Opening the top drawer, she fingered her way to the T section and found the empty "TESTS—Second Semester" hanging folder and slid the thick envelope into the vacant space. She smiled and let out a satisfied sigh. Crime was proving to be both easy and lucrative. Now all she had to do was—

"What you're doing is wrong." A voice spoke from the door connecting an adjoining office. Startled, Emma turned to see Mrs. Kellor standing across the room, empty mug in her hand.

Emma started to speak, but the teacher lifted her hand for silence. "I know it seems like the smart thing to do," the teacher continued. "Get the best of the mean school system, score high grades you didn't earn, perhaps make a few bucks. But your actions will cost you dearly in the long run. And, what about those who take advantage of your misdeeds—the students who pass tests without knowing what they should know about science? Are you doing them a great service, or are you setting them up for future failure as well?"

The woman placed her mug on the edge of her desk. "Seems you have a choice, Emma. You can do what's right and turn yourself in, or you can try to lie your way out of it—making a bad situation worse. You can't be good and bad at the same time. You can't be honest and dishonest simultaneously. Being good—doing the right thing—will, in time, remove the bad from your life. But being bad—doing what you're doing—will ultimately chase all that's good away. It's up to you which will happen."

With that, Mrs. Kellor turned and walked out the door, leaving Emma alone at the file cabinet, hands still resting atop the open drawer.

Luke 16:1–13

Jesus said to His disciples, "A wealthy business owner had a manager who had been accused of cheating. So the owner called him in and said, 'What's this I hear about you? Let's check the records. If it's true, I'll have to let you go.'

"The manager said to himself, 'If I lose my job, what am I going to do? I'm too old to dig ditches. And I don't want to beg for food. I know what I'll do! I'll quickly do some favors for people; then they'll be my friends when I need them.'

"So he called in those who owed the company money and said to the first one, 'How much do you owe?' The man said, 'A hundred gallons of olive oil.' The manager said, 'Let's make it fifty.'

"He asked the next one, 'How much do you owe?' The man said, 'One thousand bushels of wheat.' The manager said, 'Let's make it 800.'

"When the business owner heard about it, he called the manager in and complimented him on being wise enough to think about his future. Then he fired him for his dishonesty. People plan ahead for this life, but not for the next life."

Then Jesus said to the Pharisees, "You need to plan ahead for the next life, just as you plan for your future here. Those who are dishonest in little things will be dishonest in big things.

"If you can't be trusted to manage someone else's money, how can you be trusted to manage spiritual things? If you can't be trusted at one job, how can you expect someone else to hire you?

"No servant can obey two masters. He'll have to decide which one he loves more and serve him. You too will have to decide. You can't serve God and be a slave to money at the same time."

Parable 21—Two Masters

Choices. I have to make them every day: what to eat, where to go, what to say, when to study, when to play. The list is long. But some choices are more important than others. Some have *eternal* consequences.

1. Look at this list of three important choices we all make and think about the consequences:

   - I will eat unhealthy foods. This could make me

   _____ .

   - I will not study for tomorrow's test. This could make me

   _____ .

   - I will hang out with unkind people. This could make me

   _____ .

2. Look at this list of three important choices we all make and think about the consequences:

   - I will eat healthy foods. This could make me

   _____ .

   - I will study for tomorrow's test. This could make me

   _____ .

   - I will hang out with kind people. This could make me

   _____ .

3. Even though God loves me no matter what choice I make, some choices can bring consequences into my life that are unpleasant or even scary. Can you think of one?

   _____

4. God wants me to make choices that He can bless. Can you think of one?

   _____

5. I really have just one major choice to make: Am I going to serve God or am I going to serve the devil? What would you recommend and why?

_____

_____

Persistent Pete

LUKE 18:1–8

Pete, like some fifth graders, discovered that he wasn't all that fond of school. Oh he didn't mind the teachers, he was fond of his classmates, and he especially enjoyed being on the school soccer team. But what he *didn't* like was all that studying.

Unlike the previous school years, he was now expected to read lots of books, look up tons of stuff on the computer, and then remember what he'd read and looked up so that he could share his newfound knowledge on the endless tests and quizzes crowding into his up 'til now simple life. He determined that, if he wasn't expected to learn anything, school would be an absolute blast.

Pete's grades began to suffer. He dropped from being a B student to a C student and then to a D+ student. He parents noticed the slide and said, "Pete, it's time you get serious about school." He responded by saying, "I *am* serious about school. It's all that learning that's getting in the way."

He knew his parents were right. But how do you get serious about something you don't enjoy?

Pete was an all-or-nothing kind of guy. He never did anything halfway. He always completed what he started, even if the end result wasn't exactly what it was supposed to be. Once he lost the directions to the model Sherman tank he was building and ended up making what looked like a model spaceship. The doghouse he attempted to build for his dog Max reminded people of a beaver lodge, except the door was on top. Max loved it.

So when he realized that studying and learning stuff at school was becoming a problem, he set out to fix the situation in his own, all-or-nothing style.

First, he made a new friend. Arthur Thompson was the kind of kid nobody wanted to sit with during lunch. But he happened to be the smartest person in the fifth grade. Pete knew that behind those thick, wire-rim glasses, wayward red hair, and fingernails-on-blackboard laugh was someone who could explain why birds migrate, where Argentina was, and how to spell words that no one ever used in normal conversation.

He was also always available—especially during lunchtime. Pete started flopping down beside him in the cafeteria and asking him questions between bites of peanut butter and jelly sandwich and carrot sticks. Arthur knew the answer to *everything*.

Then there was Sarah, Pete's baby sister. Mother asked him to watch her so she could work uninterrupted in her home office for a couple hours after school. At first, Pete complained. Then he realized that watching Sarah meant sitting in a chair and, literally, *watching Sarah* play with her dollies on the living room rug. This was the perfect opportunity for him to read some of the many books that the teachers at school felt he needed to read—*and* get paid a dollar an hour at the same time. Win, win!

Little by little, Pete found time to do all the studying he needed. Going somewhere in the car? Take along his science book and learn how penguins survive in the bitter cold. Time for a little TV watching? Instead of cartoons or some silly sitcom, he chose a channel with lots of documentaries about things he was studying—such as what life is like in Argentina. And wonder of wonders, he discovered that if something he heard in class wasn't clear to him, the teacher didn't seem to mind saying it again just to him after class let out. It was like they *enjoyed* the opportunity!

The result of all of this persistent chasing after better grades was better grades. Pete quickly became a C student, then a B student. And imagine his surprise when a report card announced to the world that he'd attained the lofty status of an A student! Like it or not, he'd become another Arthur Thompson.

The biggest lesson Pete learned was that one should never give up on a goal. It may take a bit of work and creativity, but everything is possible—even for someone who doesn't enjoy learning.

Luke 18:1–8

Jesus told His disciples a story to encourage them to pray. He said, "In a certain city there was a very mean judge. In the same town there was a widow who pleaded with him to settle her case so that people wouldn't take her property.

"The judge kept refusing to take her case. Finally he said, 'I'm not afraid of anyone, but that widow keeps bothering me and is wearing me out. Next time she comes, I'll see to it that she gets justice.' "

Then Jesus said, "Why do you think this mean judge finally gave in? God isn't like that. He doesn't answer prayers just to stop people from bothering Him. Even though sometimes He waits before answering, He is eager to help anyone who comes to Him.

"The time will come when God will right all wrongs. But when I come back, how many people will I find who will still have faith and love God?"

Parable 22—Persistent Pete

"Never give up." Good advice, if what you're wanting to do is helpful to yourself and the world in general. Some things are worth fighting for. Some things aren't. God wants us to know the difference.

1. Name three things in life that need our constant attention—such as our health:

   - _____
   - _____
   - _____

2. Name three things in life that receive far more attention than they deserve—such as watching television:

   - _____
   - _____
   - _____

3. What do you do when you get tired and stop doing something meaningful—but you know that it's important for you to keep doing it? How do you motivate yourself to stay at it?

   _____

4. Will living in heaven with Jesus be worth the effort? What about heaven excites you the most?

   _____

5. When you think about the life of Jesus here on earth, were there times when He wanted to give up and return to His Father? What made Him stay? What does that teach us?

PARABLE 23

The Right Man for the Job

LUKE 18:9–14

P erry could almost feel the handlebar grips in his tightly closed palms and the pressure of the rapidly rotating pedals under the soles of his feet as he ran toward the hardware store. *What would it be like,* he wondered to himself, *to race down the street on his brand new, super lightweight, cherry apple red bicycle with the steel frame, twenty-one-speed drive train with a Shimano rear derailleur, alloy caliper brakes and levers, high-performance 700c tires, and a Vitesse racing seat?*

His dream machine was waiting for him at the nearby bike shop. All he needed to bring it home was a mere $168.38 with tax. That's why getting this job was so important. He figured if he worked hard and did all that was demanded of him, the bike could be his by the end of the summer. Then he could speed around town like a king on his favorite mount, enjoying the fresh air and looks of envy coming from his friends at every turn. Yes, he just had to get this job. He just *had* to.

"You two young men are the only ones applying for the stockroom position here at Abby's Hardware," Mr. Abby said, looking down at Perry and Jake—a boy that Perry had never met. "This job requires hard work, organizational skills, and a dedication to the needs of customers," he added. "Do you think you two possess those qualities?"

Perry and his competition nodded yes.

"OK," Mr. Abby said, addressing the first applicant. "Tell me why you are the right person for this job."

"I'm glad you asked that question," Jake said eagerly, rising to his feet. "I'm a very hard worker and, unlike other teenagers in the area, I am not afraid to get my hands dirty and do what needs to be done. As a matter of fact, I can work better and faster and I am more organized than any other person in this county—possibly the whole state. You'd be smart to hire me because I know hardware perfectly. Tools, paints, stuff like that. I've seen my dad use them all. And if a customer comes in with a question, I can set them straight fast! I can show them where they're wrong and how to do the job right. Yes, sir, I'm your guy, Mr. Abby. Hire me and I'll prove it to you so fast you'll be amazed and probably want to promote me to assistant manager in two weeks. I'll boost your sales and bring in new customers because people will see how smart I am."

"Well," Mr. Abby said. "You certainly have enthusiasm and a high degree of confidence in yourself."

Jake beamed and shot a quick "You're toast" look at Perry. "I'm not like other guys," he said, lifting his chin just slightly as he sat down. "I'm the best."

"And you, young man," Mr. Abby said, addressing Perry. "What can you bring to this job?"

Perry thought for a long moment, then spoke slowly. "I'm a hard worker too. At least that's what Mrs. Thompson says. Each summer I mow her lawn and weed her flowers. I've also helped my dad fix things around the house and am learning what tool does what. I know the difference between pliers and needle-nose pliers and what they're for. Dad taught me. And my mom says my room could pass inspection in the army, so I guess I'm organized. I know most of the people here in town, since I deliver papers to them each day. They're very friendly and always wave and smile at me."

The boy paused. "I guess what I'm saying is that I may not be the best in the county. But I'm willing to learn what to do and how to do it. I'll be on time and work hard. If you teach me how, I know I can be a good worker for you."

* * * * *

Two months later, Perry was able to ride to his job at the hardware store on his brand-new, cherry apple red bicycle with the steel frame, twenty-one-speed drivetrain with a Shimano rear derailleur, and alloy caliper brakes.

Luke 18:9–14

Then Jesus told another story. He wanted to show them that doing everything just right but looking down on other people does not please God.

He said, "Two men went to the Temple to pray. One was a priest and the other a tax collector. The priest went up front and prayed, 'Dear God, I thank You that I am not like people who lie, steal, cheat, and collect taxes from us to give to the Romans. I fast twice a week and bring You an honest tithe.'

"But the tax collector stayed in the back. He bowed his head and prayed, 'O God, I know I'm a sinner. Please help me!'

"This tax collector was forgiven, but not the priest. People who do good things for selfish reasons try to make themselves look great. But those who admit their sinfulness and humble themselves are great in God's eyes and will get the help they need to do better."

Parable 23—The Right Man for the Job

God needs confident Christians in His spiritual army. There are some days when I don't feel like a good soldier. So does God kick me out? No. He sends me back to boot camp (the Bible) for some additional training.

1. How does the world measure success?

   _____

   _____

2. How does God measure success?

   _____

   _____

3. Which success matters most and why?

   _____

   _____

4. What three things should we do whenever we feel less than confident as we try to be valuable soldiers in God's army of love? (Hint: You'll find that Jesus did these three things often when He was here on earth.)

   • _____

   • _____

   • _____

5. False pride (pride built on what we wish we were) can only get us so far in this world. All it needs to flourish are words. True pride (pride built on successful actions) can get us a lot further. What's the best way for you and me to turn our false pride into true pride?

   _____

Happy Harvest

MARK 4:26–29

Mr. Anderson cleared his throat and shifted slightly on his too-small chair as Miss Cooper, the English teacher at his daughter's elementary school, glanced through a small stack of papers on her desk. She silently read the words neatly printed on each page as the sound of running feet and slamming lockers echoed along the hallways beyond the closed classroom door.

"Is my Lizzie in trouble?" the man asked quietly.

Miss Cooper lowered the last page and smiled. "No, Mr. Anderson, Elizabeth is not in trouble. I . . . I just wanted to meet the man who made the soil."

Mr. Anderson blinked. "Made the soil? What do you mean?"

The teacher leaned back in her chair and thought for a long moment. Then she spoke. "Last week, your daughter was bullied by a group of children in the hallway. They said some unkind things about her, about how she doesn't have a mom and her dad works as a garbage collector."

Mr. Anderson nodded. "Well, that's true. Lizzie's mom died late last year, and I do work for the sanitation department."

"They said you live in a rundown apartment by the filling station at the edge of town," Miss Cooper added.

"Yes," the man agreed. "We're hoping to find a better place someday, but my wife's illness drained our savings. It may be a while."

The teacher paused, almost afraid to say her next words. "And . . . and they said that you have a drinking problem."

Mr. Anderson turned and glanced out the window. "I did," he admitted. "But I've been sober for more than three years now. I wish more people knew that."

"So," Miss Cooper pressed, "aren't you angry at the bullies? Don't you want to defend yourself or defend your daughter?"

"From what?" the man asked. "The truth? Those bullies were right. Why should I get mad at words that are true? Besides my Lizzie knows me. She knows my past. But she also knows something those bullies don't know. I love her more than anything in this world and I will work hard to put a roof over her head and food on her table. I will collect garbage and dig ditches and do whatever it takes to care for her needs. If some bullies think that's something to laugh at or make fun of, what do I care? My Lizzie understands that sometimes life can be unkind and embarrassing. But she knows my heart and that's what's most important."

A smile spread across Miss Cooper's face as she folded her hands and placed them atop the stack of papers. "And there it is."

Mr. Anderson frowned. "There *what* is, Miss Cooper?" he asked.

"The soil."

"I don't understand," the man stated.

The English teacher stood and walked to the window. Beyond the glass she could see several grades of children at recess, some enjoying a game of soccer, others sitting quietly in the shade of the big oaks. "Do you garden?" she asked.

"No ma'am," the man stated, confused at the teacher's words.

"Well, I do. And, I've learned a lot about soil. If I want my seeds to grow, I need to make sure the soil is healthy and filled with good nutrients. I can have the best seeds, but if my soil isn't of good quality, those seeds will die."

She turned to face her visitor. "Mr. Anderson, your daughter has been growing up in some wonderful soil. You've taught her not to be afraid of the truth, to accept criticism from mean children who don't know the whole story, and to be proud of a dad who is doing the best he can under sad circumstances." She smiled. "That's why she didn't get angry at those bullies. That's why she studies hard and is kind to others here at school, especially those whose families are struggling. I just wanted to tell you how proud I am of Elizabeth. I'm also proud of you, Mr. Anderson. Because of you, she will enjoy a happy harvest in her life. I just know it."

Through the window came the muffled sound of children at play. The man recognized one particular cheery voice—and smiled.

Mark 4:26–29

"The kingdom of heaven is like a man who has planted good seed. He works hard and has confidence that the seed will spring up and grow, even if he doesn't know how.

"He knows that the soil will produce a harvest. First, the seed sprouts; then there's the little stalk; then the head; and finally the full head of grain. Then he calls in workers to help him bring in the harvest."

Parable 24—Happy Harvest

I love to watch a garden grow. Seeds become new plants. New plants become ripe plants. Ripe plants become a healthy dinner for me to enjoy. But seeds, all by themselves, don't do anything. They need help.

1. What are the three things that seeds need in order to grow up to be a ripe plant?

    • _____

    • _____

    • _____

2. Of course, any gardener will tell you that there are a few critters and some unwelcome plants (weeds) that will try to destroy your garden. The trick is to get rid of the critters and weeds without hurting the growing plants. Why is it not the best idea to spray powerful chemicals on your plants?

    _____

3. The best way to rid your garden of pesky plants and critters is to carefully take them out by hand. It is hard work. But why is it the best way?

    _____

4. What does soil need to be healthy? (You might want to check with a gardener for the complete answer to this question.)

    _____

5. What do we all need to be spiritually healthy? (You might want to check with your parents, teachers, or pastor for the complete answer to this question.)

    _____

One Wolf, Two Skunks, and a Rattlesnake

LUKE 11:33–36

W hat happened next?" Sarah wanted to know.

Mario leaned in close and spoke just above a whisper. "He shot him dead right then and there. *Bam*. Dead!"

"Who got shot dead?" Grandpa called out, entering the room.

Mario laughed. "Oh, it's not real, Grandpa," he assured the old man as he sank into his favorite chair by the crackling fire. "It's just a TV show we've been watching."

"Are people shooting people dead all the time on this program?" Grandpa wanted to know.

Sarah giggled. "Oh no," she said. "Sometimes they get stabbed or thrown off of a cliff. One time the bad guy was tossed into a pond with a hungry crocodile in it. Let's just say the crock had a special guest for lunch."

Grandpa frowned. "Did I ever tell you about the time when I left the garage door open?"

Sarah and Mario blinked, taken back by the sudden change of subject. "Uh, no," they chorused. "But we'd like to hear it."

Grandpa always had such amazing adventures to share. They settled themselves at the old man's feet and waited for their favorite storyteller to take a couple sips of his favorite hot tea. Then he got a familiar, faraway look in his eyes.

"I was probably Sarah's age, and we were living on the farm in west Texas," the old man began. "Dad had to go to town one afternoon and said he'd be getting back late. He told me to be sure to close the garage door when I finished riding my bike. I said I would. Except I didn't. I plum forgot. I put my bike away and then hurried out to the barn to do some chores before heading in after dark to attack my homework. I failed to notice that the garage door was wide open, letting in the night air.

"Later that evening, a storm came through—a real gully washer—and the wind blew something fierce. Knocked the power out completely. Since it was late anyway, I decided to go to bed and was fast asleep when Dad came into my room and said, 'Get up. I've got something to show you.'

"So I followed him down the hall, out the front door, and over to the garage resting near the old maple. Dad told me to stand by the tree and he shone his very bright flashlight toward the garage. That's when I remembered that I had forgotten to close the door. I was about to apologize for my mistake, when I noticed that the entire inside of the garage was covered with puddles of water and blown leaves and branches."

"I'll bet he was mad," Mario said with an understanding nod.

"Oh but that wasn't all," Grandpa continued. "In the darkness at the back of the garage, I saw two eyes glowing back at me and hear a deep growl. Then I saw two more sets of eyes shining out from the shadows. And then I heard a buzzing sound—the kind that any kid from West Texas will tell you means real trouble. Seems my open garage door had let in a lot more than rain, leaves, and limbs. My dad called out, and immediately, the biggest wolf I'd ever seen ran out into the night, followed by two very upset, frightened, and stinky skunks. Then, the source of the buzzing slithered out—the meanest-looking rattlesnake I'd ever seen."

"Wow," Sarah breathed. "What did you do?"

"Well, after we checked for other critters and found none, I closed the garage door."

The old man studied his two grandchildren. "We have to be careful when we leave doors open around the farm. We also have to be careful when we leave our minds open to sights and sounds that might harm us—things that make terrible events seem funny or portray violent acts as innocent adventures. Know what I mean?"

Mario and Sarah nodded slowly as the full meaning of the story sank in. They determined then and there to be a lot more selective when it came to the television programs they watched because one never knows what creatures may choose to hide inside the mind.

Luke 11:33–36

"No one lights a candle and then hides it, but he holds it up so everyone in the house can see. Your eyes are like candles. You see what you're looking for. When you look for what's good, that's what you'll see. When you look for what's wrong, you'll see that, too.

"If you keep looking for what's wrong, soon you'll be unhappy, and your life will be dark. If you look for what's good, you'll be happy, and your life will shine like a lamp that gives light."

Parable 25—One Wolf, Two Skunks, and a Rattlesnake

I once had someone say to me, "You are what you eat." In other words, my body is built by what I put in it. After he said that, I cut way back on junk food. You can probably figure out why.

1. To have a fully functioning, smart brain, what do we need to fill it with?

    • _____

    • _____

    • _____

2. To have a brain that's lazy and selfish, what do we need to fill it with?

    • _____

    • _____

    • _____

3. What does the world (under the control of the devil) offer our brains? Where do we find these "gifts" from the world?

    _____

4. What does Jesus (working in partnership with God the Father) offer our brains? Where do we find these "gifts" from God?

    _____

5. What three things should we do each day that ensure that we're receiving and enjoying the most powerful "gifts" from God?

    • _____

    • _____

    • _____